KEY MATHS 9

▶ **Roma Harvey**

▶ **Gill Hewlett**

▶ **Elaine Judd**

▶ **Jo Pavey**

▶ **Maureen Sandford**

Nelson Thornes

Contents

Acknowledgements

The publishers thank the following for permission to reproduce copyright material:

Allsport: 134, 196T (Mike Powell); AKG London: 176B (Robert O'Dea); Bubbles Photo library: 200B (Roger Chester), 290L (Martin Jackson); Collections: 200T (Richard Davis), 201T (Paul Bryans), 202T (V.I), 290R (Paul Bryans), 312 (Bill Wells); Corbis Sygma: 328B (Ministry of Sound/S. Tovaig); Eye Ubiquitous: 200M (Peter Blake), 202B (Sean Aidon); John Walmsley: 194, 195, 203, 308T; www.johnbirdsall.co.uk: 201B; Martyn Chillmaid: 11, 26, 27, 29, 31, 33, 43, 44, 55, 56, 60, 67, 74, 88TL, BR, 93TL, BL, 94, 102L, 121, 150, 152, 153, 154, 155, 156, 157, 170, 196B, 207, 278, 286, 308B; PPL Limited: 1; Rex Features: 179; Sally and Richard Greenhill: 308M; Stone: 103; Sylvia Cordaiy: 176T, 209 (Patrick Partington); Topham Picture Point: 326; Travel Ink: 25 (D. Toase), 175 (Simon Reddy); TRH Pictures: 277.

The publishers have made every effort to contact copyright holders but apologise if any have been overlooked.

First published in 2000 by
Stanley Thornes (Publishers) Ltd

Reprinted in 2001 by:
Nelson Thornes Ltd
Delta Place
27 Bath Road
CHELTENHAM
GL53 7TH
United Kingdom

01 02 03 04 / 10 9 8 7 6 5 4 3 2

A catalogue record for this book is available from the British Library.

ISBN 0 7487 5306 0

Original design concept by Studio Dorel
Cover design by John Christopher, Design Works
Artwork by Oxford Designers and Illustrators and Peters and Zabransky
Cartoons by Clinton Banbury
Typeset by Tech Set Ltd
Printed and bound in Italy by G. Canale & C.S.p.A., Borgaro T.se, Turin

1 Area

QUESTIONS

The *Cutty Sark* is an old merchant sailing ship which is kept at Greenwich on the River Thames. It was built in 1869 with a total area of sails of 32 000 square feet or 2972 square metres.

1 Counting shapes

Malcolm is going to change the shape of his patio.
He wants it to be the same area.
He must use all the slabs in his new design.

Example **a** Draw a **rectangular** patio.
Use all 16 slabs.

1	2	3	4	5	6	7	8
9	10	11	12	13	14	15	16

Malcolm could have a rectangular patio like this.

b Draw a **different** shape using 16 slabs.
At least **one whole side** must touch the next slab

Like this ✓ or this ✓ but **not** ✗ or ✗

1	2	3	4		
5	6	7	8	9	10
11	12	13	14	15	16

Malcolm could have this shape.
This is not a rectangle.
It is another shape.

Exercise 1:1

1 This patio has 10 slabs.

1	2	3	4	5	6	7	8	9	10

Using 10 slabs, draw on squared paper

a a different rectangular patio

b two other patio designs, any shape.

2 Using 20 slabs, draw all possible rectangular patios.

Area   **Area** is measured using squares.

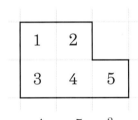

1 cm

1 cm

Area 1 cm²

1	2
3	4	5

Area 5 cm²

Exercise 1:2

1 These shapes are made with centimetre squares.
Find the area of each shape.

a

c

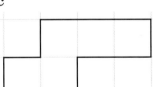

e

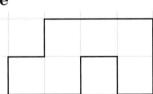

b

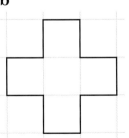

d

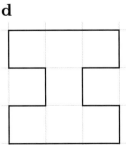

f

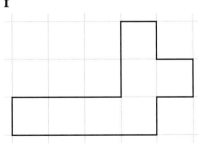

Two half squares put together make one whole square.

$\frac{1}{2}$ square $\quad$ $\frac{1}{2}$ square $\quad$ 1 cm^2

Examples Find the area of each shape in cm^2.

a

Whole squares $= 2$
One $\frac{1}{2}$ square $= \frac{1}{2}$

Total area $= \underline{2\frac{1}{2}\,\text{cm}^2}$

b

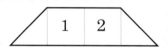

Whole squares $\quad\quad = 2$
Two $\frac{1}{2}$ squares $(\frac{1}{2} + \frac{1}{2}) = 1$

Total area $\quad\quad\quad = \underline{3\,\text{cm}^2}$

c

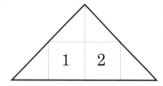

Whole squares $\quad\quad\quad\quad = 2$
Four $\frac{1}{2}$ squares $(\frac{1}{2} + \frac{1}{2}) + (\frac{1}{2} + \frac{1}{2}) = 2$

Total area $\quad\quad\quad\quad = \underline{4\,\text{cm}^2}$

 2 Find the area of these shapes in cm^2.
You can write on the helpsheet, **not** in the book.

a

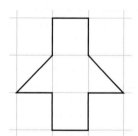

c

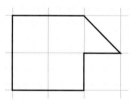

e

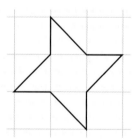

b

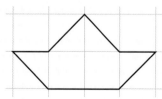

d

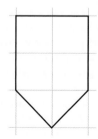

f

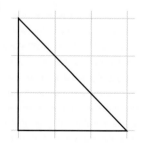

The area of some shapes can only be **estimated** and not worked out exactly.

Example   What is the area of this pond?

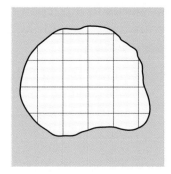

To **estimate** the area, first count the **whole** squares.

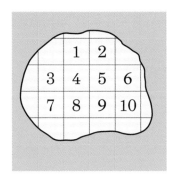

Then count the squares that are **more than half** full. (*Ignore any squares that are less than half full.*)

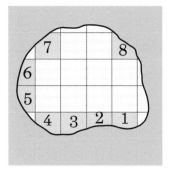

There are 10 whole squares.

There are 8 of these.

An estimate of the area of the pond is $10 + 8 = 18$ squares

Exercise 1:3

1   Estimate the area of each pond.
Write on the helpsheet, **not** in the book.

a

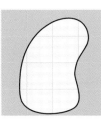

c

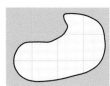

b

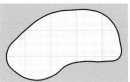

d

Lorna works in a garden centre.
She says a pond can take 2 fish
for every square.

Example   How many fish will
this pond take?

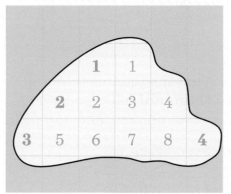

There are **8** whole squares.
There are **4** which are more than
half full.
Estimated area **8** + **4** = 12 squares

2 fish × 12 squares
= 24 fish

 2

2 (1)   Estimate the area of each pond.
(2)   Work out how many fish can live there.
Remember each square can take 2 fish.

a

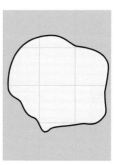

b

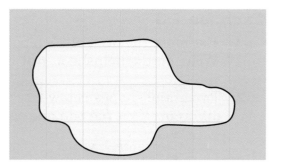

You are a garden designer.

On squared paper draw some ponds of your own. Work out the
number of fish that can live in each of your ponds.

Example   Areas are added when shapes are placed together.

square   triangle

area 4 cm²   area 2 cm²

Pat has stuck two
shapes together.

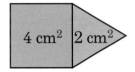

The area of Pat's new shape is $4 + 2 = 6\,\text{cm}^2$

Exercise 1:4

1 Pat has made some other shapes.
Find the area of each one.

a 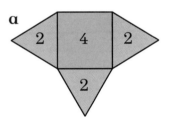   **b** 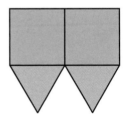   **c**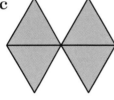

Area $4 + 2 + 2 + 2 = \ldots \text{cm}^2$

2 Two of the shapes below have the same area, one is
different. Find the odd one out.

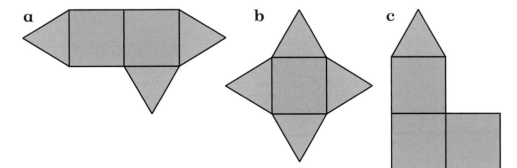

3 The rectangle and the square shown below are not drawn to scale.

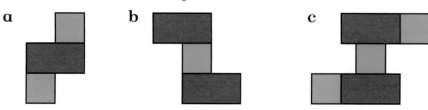

rectangle   square

area 7 cm^2 area 3 cm^2

Find the area of each shape.

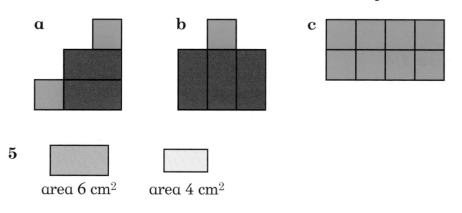

a   b   c

4 Find the odd one out from the areas of the 3 shapes below.

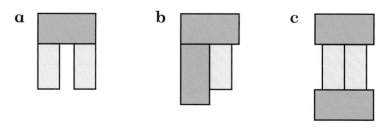

a   b   c

5

area 6 cm^2 area 4 cm^2

Find the area of each shape.

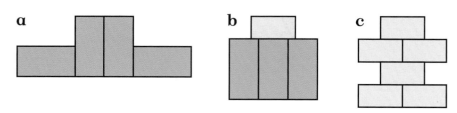

a   b   c

6 Find the odd one out from the areas of the 3 shapes below.

a   b   c

7   hexagon   parallelogram

area 10 cm²   area 5 cm²

Find the area of each shape.

a 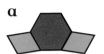   b 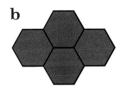   c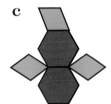

8   Find the odd one out from the 3 shapes below.

a   b    c

Exercise 1:5

Cara has drawn these shapes.
The area of each shape is given.

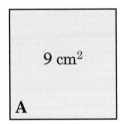   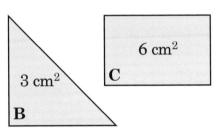

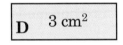

1   **1**   Cut out the shapes on the worksheet.

Example   **a** Which **two** shapes can be
used to fill this rectangle?

b What is the area of this
rectangle?

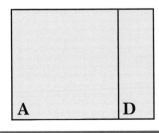

a Answer: shapes A and D.

b Area of rectangle = shape A + shape D
= 9 + 3
= 12 cm²

W 1   **2**   Use the cut out shapes to answer these questions.

a

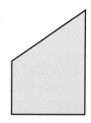

  (1)   Which 2 shapes fit?
  (2)   Find the area.

c

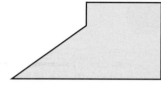

  (1)   Which 3 shapes fit?
  (2)   Find the area.

b

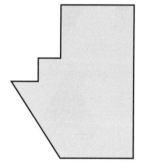

  (1)   Which 4 shapes fit?
  (2)   Find the area.

d

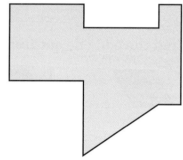

  (1)   Fit in all 5 shapes.
  (2)   Find the area.

3   Cara has made a pattern with her shapes.

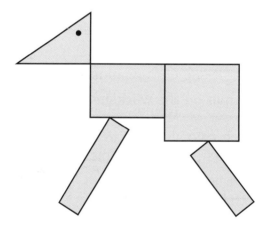

  a What is the area of Cara's pattern?

  b Use the shapes to make your own pattern.
      Stick it into your book.

  c Write down the area of your pattern.

2 Areas of rectangles and parallelograms

Each row on this sheet has 5 stamps

There are 2 rows.

There are $5 \times 2 = 10$ stamps altogether.

Example

a How many squares are there in each row?
   Answer: 4 squares.

b How many rows are there?
   Answer: 3 rows.

c How many squares are there altogether?
   Answer: $4 \times 3 = 12$ squares altogether.

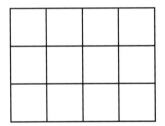

Exercise 1:6

1 For each rectangle say (1) how many squares there are in each row.
   (2) how many rows there are.
   (3) how many squares there are altogether.
   Write ... $\times$ ... = ... cm^2

a 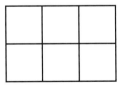   b 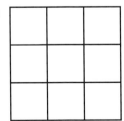   c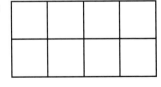

Squares in a row $\times$ number of rows = total number of squares

Area of a rectangle
        = *length* × *width*
    or $A = l \times w$

length

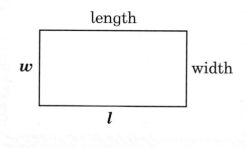

w   width

l

Units

cm

cm^2 cm

centimetre squared

Example
Calculate the area of this rectangle.

Area = length × width
    = 5 × 4
    = 20 cm^2

5 cm

4 cm

---

2 Calculate the area of these rectangles.
    Write in the units.

a

3 cm

5 cm

Area = *l* × *w*

    = ... × ...

    = ... cm^2

c

6 cm

5 cm

b

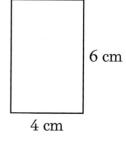

6 cm

4 cm

d

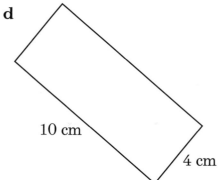

10 cm

4 cm

Example   Are the areas of these magazine pictures the same or
different?

   3 cm

   4 cm

5 cm

4 cm

Area = 5 × 3 = 15 cm²   Area = 4 × 4 = 16 cm²

The areas are different.

3   Are these areas the same or different?
Show your workings.

a      5 cm   and   6 cm

4 cm

    4 cm

b      4 cm   and   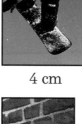   8 cm

4 cm

   2 cm

c      6 cm   and      7 cm

10 cm   9 cm

4 From a magazine find two **different shaped** pictures that have the same area.

Stick them in your book and write down the measurements.

Metres   Large items are measured
in **metres**.
Use 4 one metre sticks
or 4 pieces of string 1 metre long.
Mark out a square on the floor.
This is the area of one square
metre.

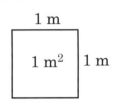

1 m

1 m² | 1 m

metre squared

---

5 For each of the following items, write down if **cm²** or **m²** would be best to use when finding the area in real life.

A

Dinner plate

C

Hockey pitch

E

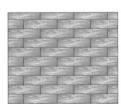

Classroom floor

B

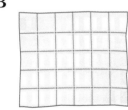

Tablecloth

D

Hand

F

Postage stamp

In real life,

a Which has the smallest area?

b Which has the largest area?

c Put them in order of area, smallest first.

Exercise 1:7

The items below are large.
They are measured in metres.
You may use a calculator.

1 What is the area of the pool?
Area = $l \times w$
Area = ... $\times$ ......
Area = ... m^2

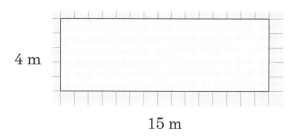

4 m

15 m

2 What is the area of the wall?

3 m

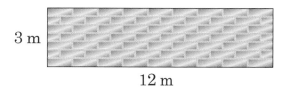

12 m

3 What is the area of the pitch?

50 m

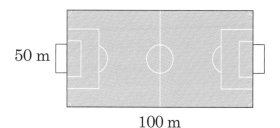

100 m

4 This warehouse block stands on a corner.
Two sides and the top need painting.
Find the area of:

a the front of the building   ....

b the side of the building   ....

c the top of the building   ....

Total area to be painted   ....

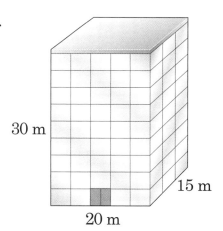

30 m

15 m

20 m

Example   John sells pictures.
Find the area of this picture.

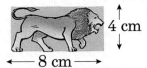

4 cm

8 cm

Area $= 8 \times 4$
$\quad\quad = 32\,\text{cm}^2$

Use the table to work out the cost.

Area of picture	Cost
Up to 50 cm²	£5
Over 50 cm²	£8

$32\,\text{cm}^2$ is less than $50\,\text{cm}^2$
Cost $= £5$

Exercise 1:8

1 Work out the cost of these pictures.

a

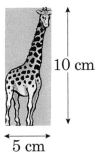

10 cm

5 cm

b

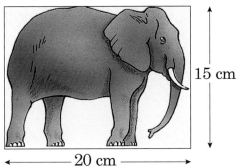

15 cm

20 cm

2 Lisa makes bookends for presents.
She buys wood in squares.

Area of wood	Cost
Less than 200 cm²	50p
200 to 600 cm²	£1
Over 600 cm²	£2

How much will Lisa pay for these pieces of wood?

a

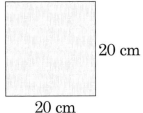

20 cm

20 cm

b

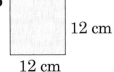

12 cm

12 cm

c

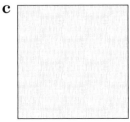

25 cm

25 cm

16

Area of a parallelogram	A parallelogram can be changed to a rectangle.

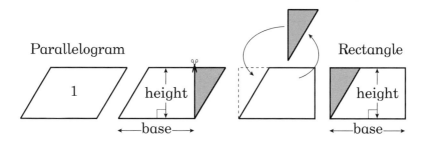

Area of a parallelogram = area of a rectangle
= base × height
The **height** must always be at **right angles** to the base.

Exercise 1:9

1 a Cut out parallelogram 1 from the worksheet and stick it into your book.

b Make a rectangle from the other parallelogram. Stick it into your book and label it 'Rectangle'.

c Copy into your book

Area of a parallelogram = area of a rectangle
= base × height

2 For these parallelograms write down the length of
i the base   **ii** the height

a

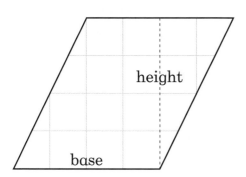

b

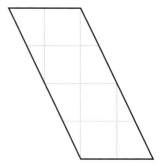

Example   Find the area of this parallelogram.

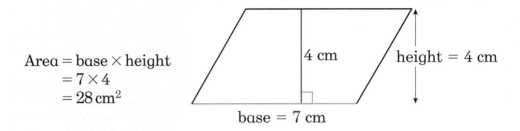

Area = base × height
    = 7 × 4
    = 28 cm²

4 cm

height = 4 cm

base = 7 cm

Exercise 1:10

Find the areas of these parallelograms.

1

8 cm

10 cm

3

3 cm

11 cm

2

12 cm

5 cm

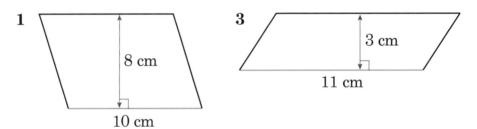

4

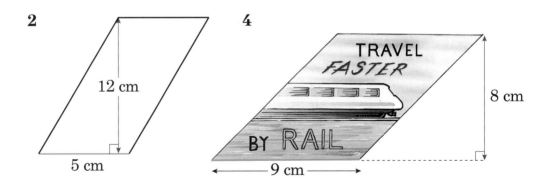

TRAVEL
FASTER

BY RAIL

8 cm

9 cm

3 **5** Hannah paints logos on sweatshirts.
The table shows how much they cost.

Area of logo	Cost
Under 10 cm^2	50p
10 to 15 cm^2	£1
Over 15 cm^2	£2

For each of these logos (1) measure the base
(2) measure the height
(3) write down the area
(4) write down the cost.

a

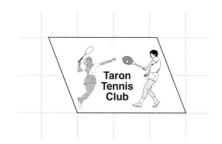

b

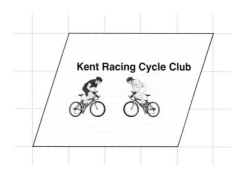

c

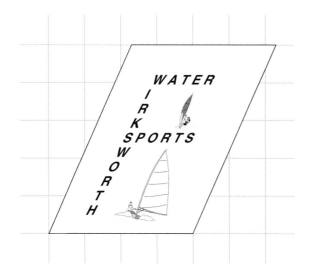

3   Areas of triangles

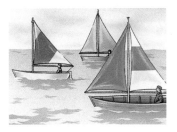

The bigger the sail area the faster the yacht will go.

Area of right angled triangles

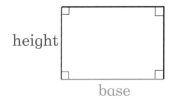

Area of rectangle
= **base** × **height**

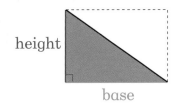

Area of the shaded triangle is **half** the area of the rectangle.

Area of triangle $= \dfrac{\textbf{base} \times \textbf{height}}{2}$

Example Find the area of this triangle.

$$\begin{aligned}
\text{Area of triangle} &= \frac{\textbf{base} \times \textbf{height}}{2} \\
&= \frac{6 \times 4}{2} \\
&= 24 \div 2 \\
&= 12 \,\text{cm}^2
\end{aligned}$$

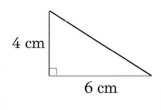

4 cm

6 cm

Exercise 1:11

Find the areas of these triangles.

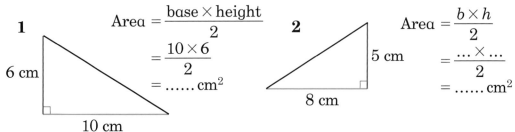

1

6 cm

10 cm

Area $= \dfrac{\text{base} \times \text{height}}{2}$

$= \dfrac{10 \times 6}{2}$

$= \ldots\ldots \text{cm}^2$

2

5 cm

8 cm

Area $= \dfrac{b \times h}{2}$

$= \dfrac{\ldots \times \ldots}{2}$

$= \ldots\ldots \text{cm}^2$

(The base is not always at the bottom.)

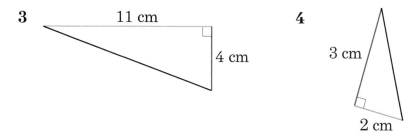

3 11 cm 4 cm

4 3 cm 2 cm

| **Area of other shaped triangles** | Height measurement must always be taken at **right angles** to the base. |

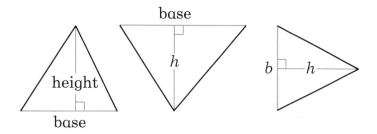

base

height base

h

b h

Example Find the area of this triangle.

$$\text{Area of triangle} = \frac{\textbf{base} \times \textbf{height}}{2}$$
$$= \frac{8 \times 6}{2}$$
$$= 48 \div 2$$
$$= 24 \text{ cm}^2$$

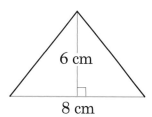

6 cm

8 cm

Exercise 1:12

Find the areas of these triangles.

1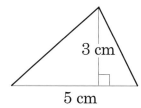

3 cm

5 cm

2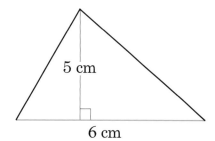

5 cm

6 cm

3

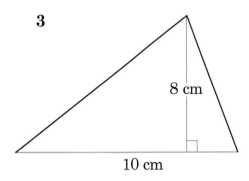

8 cm

10 cm

4

7 cm

4 cm

5 a Which sail has the larger area?

Explain how you know.

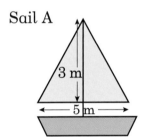

Sail A

3 m

5 m

Sail B

4 m

3 m

6 For each triangle
   (1) measure the base and height.
   (2) find the area.

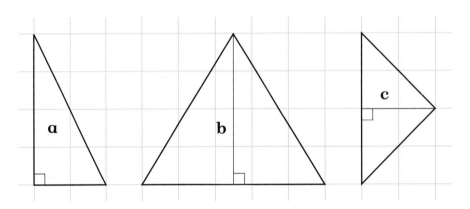

a

b

c

7 What is special about the areas of the 3 triangles below?

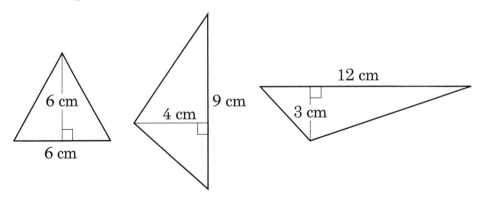

6 cm

6 cm

4 cm

9 cm

12 cm

3 cm

1 Write down the area of each shape.

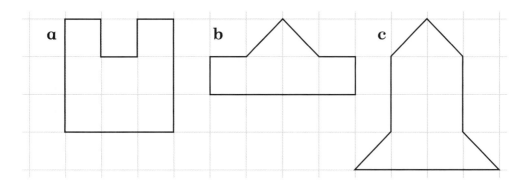

a   b   c

2 The area of the square is $9\,\text{cm}^2$. The area of the triangle is $5\,\text{cm}^2$.

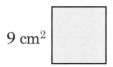 $9\,\text{cm}^2$  $5\,\text{cm}^2$

Find the area of each shape.

a   b   c

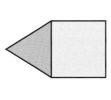
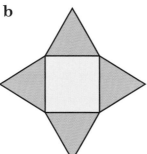
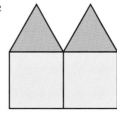

3 Find the areas of these rectangles.

a   b   c

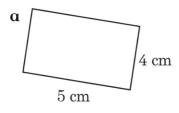   4 cm

5 cm

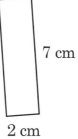   7 cm

2 cm

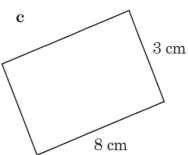   3 cm

8 cm

4 Estimate the area of this pond.

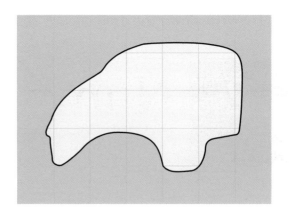

5 Would you use **cm²** or **m²** to measure the area of
a a playground **b** a pencil case?

6 Find the areas of these parallelograms.

a

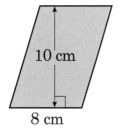

10 cm

8 cm

b

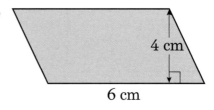

4 cm

6 cm

7 Find the areas of these triangles.

a

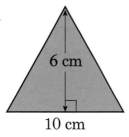

6 cm

10 cm

b

5 cm

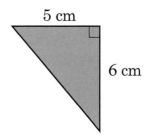

6 cm

8 **a** Find the area of each of these logos.
b Which has the smallest area?

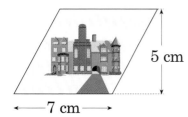

5 cm

7 cm

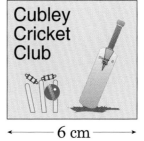

4 cm

8 cm

Cubley
Cricket
Club

6 cm

6 cm

2 Number

QUESTIONS

Before decimalisation took place in the UK in 1971 one pound sterling was made up of 20 shillings, with each shilling made up of 12 pence. How many pence were there in a pound?

The new system changed the number of pence in one pound to 100.

1 Addition and multiplication

Daniel takes three apples to a checkout.
He gets a checkout slip like this:
The apples cost 10 p each

$$10 + 10 + 10 = 30$$

APPLES	10 p
APPLES	10 p
APPLES	10 p
TOTAL	30 p

10p each

Tom buys three apples in another shop.
Tom's checkout slip looks like this:

$$3 \times 10 = 30$$

APPLES		
3 @ 10 p		30 p
TOTAL		30 p

The cost is 30 p

Exercise 2:1

 1

1 This is Lucy's checkout slip:
The *TOTAL* is torn off.

COLA	15 p
COLA	15 p
COLA	15 p
TOTAL	

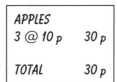

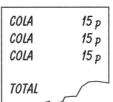

a Find Lucy's *TOTAL* by adding

$15 p + 15 p + 15 p = \ldots$

b Here is a new checkout slip for Lucy.
Fill it in.

$3 \times 15 p = \ldots$
The cost is … p

COLA		
3 @ 15 p		…
TOTAL		…

Fill in each of the checkout slips below.

(1) Find the *TOTAL* by adding.

(2) Find the *TOTAL* by multiplying.

(3) Check that the *TOTALS* are the same.

2 a

CAT FOOD	12 p
CAT FOOD	12 p
CAT FOOD	12 p
CAT FOOD	12 p
TOTAL	...

b

CAT FOOD	
4 @ 12 p	...
TOTAL	...

3 a

PIZZA	45 p
PIZZA	45 p
PIZZA	45 p
PIZZA	45 p
PIZZA	45 p
TOTAL	...

b

PIZZA	
5 @ 45 p	...
TOTAL	...

4 a

COLA	25 p
COLA	25 p
COLA	25 p
COLA	25 p
COLA	25 p
COLA	25 p
TOTAL	...

b

COLA	
6 @ 25 p	...
TOTAL	...

25p

5 a

CHICKEN	£3.99
CHICKEN	£3.99
TOTAL	...

b

CHICKEN	
2 @ £3.99	...
TOTAL	...

There is a quick way to work out the totals.

Example

    a Write this addition in numbers.
    b Write this addition as a multiplication.
    c Work out the answer.

    a 4 + 4 + 4   **b** 3 × 4   **c** 12 biscuits

Exercise 2:2

1 How many biscuits are there altogether?

    a Write this addition in numbers.
    b Write it as a multiplication.
    c Work out the answer.

2 How many cakes are there altogether?

    a Write this addition in numbers.
    b Write it as a multiplication.
    c Work out the answer.

3 How many sweets are there altogether?

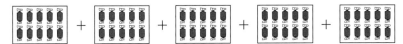

    a Write this addition in numbers.
    b Write it as a multiplication.
    c Work out the answer.

4 How many cheeses are there altogether?

    a Write this addition in numbers.
    b Write it as a multiplication.
    c Work out the answer.

Example   Work out by multiplication

$$5 + 5 + 5 + 5 + 5 + 5 = 6 \times 5 = 30$$

Exercise 2:3

For each question
a copy the addition,
b write it as a multiplication,
c work out the answer.

1 $2 + 2 + 2 = \ldots \times \ldots = \ldots$

2 $5 + 5 + 5 + 5$

3 $3 + 3 + 3 + 3$

4 $4 + 4 + 4 + 4 + 4$

5 $10 + 10 + 10 + 10 + 10$

6 $8 + 8 + 8 + 8$

7 $6 + 6 + 6 + 6 + 6$

8 $25 + 25 + 25$

Example   Find the number of mince pies in three boxes of 6 pies.

a Write the sum as an addition.
b Write it as a multiplication.
c Work out the answer.

a $6 + 6 + 6$ **b** 3×6 **c** 18

---

9 Find the number of eggs in
four boxes.
Each box has 6 eggs in it.
a Write the sum as an addition.
b Write it as a multiplication.
c Work out the answer.

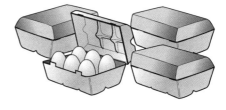

  10 Find the number of seats in
four coaches.
Each coach has 50 seats.
a Write the sum as an addition.
b Write it as a multiplication.
c Work out the answer.

2 Subtraction and division

Karen has 6 earrings.
She wants to keep them
in boxes.
Each box holds 2 earrings.

Karen puts her earrings away in the boxes.

Box 1 She has put 2 earrings away.
There are $6 - 2 = 4$ left.

Box 2 She has put 2 more earrings away.
There are $4 - 2 = 2$ left.

Box 3 She has put the last 2 earrings away.
There are $2 - 2 = 0$ left.

Karen says
$6 - 2 = 4$ 1 box
$4 - 2 = 2$ 2 boxes
$2 - 2 = 0$ 3 boxes   Karen needed three boxes.

Lynn also has 6 earrings and some boxes.
Each box holds 2 earrings.
She divides her earrings into pairs and puts them into the
boxes.

Lynn says $6 \div 2 = 3$.   Lynn has used 3 boxes. She gets the
same answer as Karen.
Karen worked it out by subtraction.
Lynn worked it out by division.
They both got the right answer.

Exercise 2:4

1 Emma has 12 rings. She wants to put them in boxes. Each box holds 3 rings. She does it like this:

1st box	$12 - 3 = 9$	left
2nd box	$9 - 3 = 6$	left
3rd box	$6 - 3 = 3$	left
4th box	$3 - 3 = 0$	left

a How many times does Emma take away 3?

b How many boxes does Emma fill?

c Check your answer with this division:

$12 \div 3 = \ldots$

2 Jason has 25 key rings. He puts them into packs. Each pack holds 5 key rings. He works out the number of packs like this:

$25 - 5 = 20$
$20 - 5 = 15$
$15 - 5 = 10$
$10 - 5 = 5$
$5 - 5 = 0$

a How many times does Jason take away 5?

b How many packs does he fill?

c Check your answer with this division:

$25 \div 5 = \ldots$

3 Ian has 20 silver coins.
He keeps them in boxes. Each box holds 4 coins.
How many boxes will he need?

a Copy these subtractions.
Take away 4 until you get 0.

$20 - 4 = 16$
$16 - 4 = \ldots$

b How many times does Ian take away 4?

c How many boxes does he fill?

d Check your answer using this division:

$20 \div 4 = \ldots$

Sometimes there is a remainder.

Example   John puts bread rolls into bags of 5 rolls. He starts with 17 rolls.

1st bag $17 - 5 = 12$ He now has 12 left.

2nd bag $12 - 5 = 7$ He now has 7 left.

3rd bag $7 - 5 = 2$ He now has 2 left over.
This is the remainder.

John can write $17 - 5 - 5 - 5 = 2$

John takes 5 away 3 times.
He is left with 2.

John can also write it as a division $17 \div 5 = 3$ remainder 2

Exercise 2:5

 3   **1**   Jason shares out 14 sausages onto some plates. Each plate holds 4 sausages.

    a How many plates does he need?

    b How many sausages will be left over?

1st plate $14 - 4 = \ldots$ He now has ... left.

2nd plate $10 - \ldots = \ldots$ He now has ... left.

3rd plate $\ldots - \ldots = \ldots$ He now has ... left over.

Jason can write $14 - \ldots - \ldots - \ldots = \ldots$
Jason takes 4 away ... times with ... left over.
He can also write it as a division $14 \div 4 = \ldots$ remainder ...

    a Jason needs ... plates.

    b There are ... sausages left over.

2 Sally has 21 doughnuts.
She puts them into boxes of 6.

   a How many boxes can Sally fill?

   b How many doughnuts will be left over?

1st box $21 - \mathbf{6} = \ldots$ She now has ... left.

2nd box   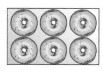 $\ldots - \ldots = \ldots$ She now has ... left.

3rd box    $\ldots - \ldots = \ldots$ She now has ... left over.

Sally can write $21 - \ldots - \ldots - \ldots = \ldots$

Sally takes **6** away ... times.
She has ... left over.

She can also write it as a division $21 \div \mathbf{6} = \ldots$ remainder ...

   a Sally can fill ... boxes.

   b There are ... doughnuts left over.

3 Peter has 18 choc bars.
He wants to put 4 choc bars into a pack.

   a How many packs can he fill?

   b How many choc bars are left over?

G 3, 4

4 Linda has 11 fizzy drinks.
She wants to put them into bags of 3.

   a How many bags of fizzy drinks
can she fill?

   b How many fizzy drinks are
left over?

3   Working without a calculator

Addition and subtraction

Example   Work these out in your head. Write down the answers.

$6 + 4 = 10$	$12 + 8 = 20$
$6 + 5 = 11$	$12 + 9 = 21$
$4 + 6 = 10$	$12 + 11 = 23$
$7 + 6 = 13$	

Exercise 2:6

Work these out in your head. Write down the answers.

1   **a** $7 + 3 =$ **b** $5 + 5 =$ **c** $8 + 2 =$
   $7 + 4 =$ $5 + 6 =$ $8 + 3 =$
   $3 + 7 =$ $5 + 7 =$ $3 + 8 =$
   $3 + 9 =$ $6 + 5 =$ $5 + 8 =$

2   **a** $9 + 11 =$ **b** $8 + 12 =$ **c** $15 + 5 =$
   $9 + 12 =$ $8 + 14 =$ $15 + 10 =$
   $10 + 11 =$ $16 + 8 =$ $15 + 12 =$

3   Find the matching pairs. Write them down like this:

$5 + 5$ ⟋⟍ $1 + 9$ $5 + 5 = 1 + 9$

$4 + 6$ $8 + 4$ $10 + 5$ $13 + 7$

$9 + 6$ $12 + 8$ $2 + 8$ $7 + 5$

'Shopkeepers' addition'

Shopkeepers can work out your change by 'counting on' from the **price** to the amount that you gave them.
'Counting on' is another way to do subtraction.

Example 1   A ruler costs 6 p. You give the shopkeeper 10 p. What is the change?

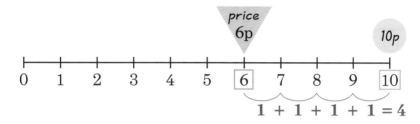

The change is 4 p.

Example 2   A pencil costs 13 p. What is the change from 20 p?

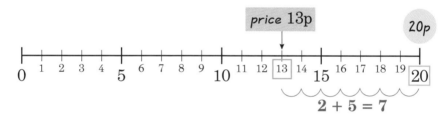

The change is 7 p.

Exercise 2:7

1   What is the change from 20 p when I spend:
  a 16 p   **b** 12 p   **c** 8 p   **d** 3 p   **e** 14 p

2   What is the change from 50 p when I spend:
  a 30 p   **b** 25 p   **c** 19 p   **d** 12 p   **e** 7 p

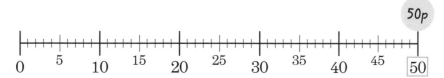

3 What is the change from £1 when I spend:

   a 76p   **b** 54p   **c** 48p   **d** 26p   **e** 32p

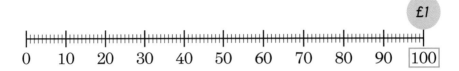

There are many ways to do subtraction in your head.

Example   52–29

You can start from 52 or 29

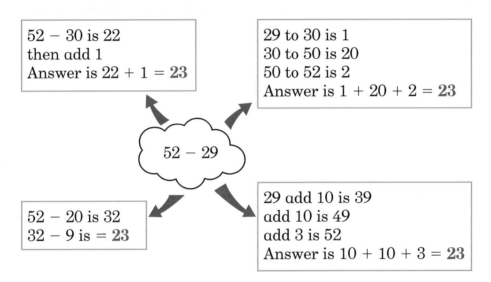

52 − 30 is 22
then add 1
Answer is 22 + 1 = **23**

29 to 30 is 1
30 to 50 is 20
50 to 52 is 2
Answer is 1 + 20 + 2 = **23**

52 − 29

52 − 20 is 32
32 − 9 is = **23**

29 add 10 is 39
add 10 is 49
add 3 is 52
Answer is 10 + 10 + 3 = **23**

4 Work out these subtractions in your head.
Use a method that works best for you.
Write down the answers.

   a 10 − 4   **j** 88 − 69
   b 20 − 15   **k** 42 − 37
   c 50 − 29   **l** 55 − 35
   d 100 − 85   **m** 100 − 64
   e 60 − 45   **n** 200 − 64
   f 50 − 42   **o** 500 − 64
   g 26 − 13   **p** 110 − 98
   h 55 − 33   **q** 110 − 78
   i 73 − 22   **r** 500 − 364

Multiplication

You can multiply without using a calculator.

Example 31×5

Set out 31×5 as
$$\begin{array}{r} 31 \\ \times\ 5 \\ \hline \\ \hline \end{array}$$
first do 5×1
$$\begin{array}{r} 31 \\ \times\ 5 \\ \hline 5 \end{array}$$
then do 5×3
$$\begin{array}{r} 31 \\ \times\ 5 \\ \hline 155 \end{array}$$

Remember! Always multiply the number in the units column first.

Tens	Units
3	1
$\times$	5
1 5	5

Exercise 2:8

Work these out.

1
a $\begin{array}{r} 23 \\ \times\ 2 \\ \hline \\ \hline \end{array}$
b $\begin{array}{r} 51 \\ \times\ 3 \\ \hline \\ \hline \end{array}$
c $\begin{array}{r} 42 \\ \times\ 4 \\ \hline \\ \hline \end{array}$
d $\begin{array}{r} 51 \\ \times\ 5 \\ \hline \\ \hline \end{array}$
e $\begin{array}{r} 74 \\ \times\ 2 \\ \hline \\ \hline \end{array}$

Sometimes you need to carry.

Example
$\begin{array}{r} 25 \\ \times\ 3 \\ \hline 5 \\ \scriptstyle 1 \end{array} \longrightarrow \begin{array}{r} 25 \\ \times\ 3 \\ \hline 75 \\ \scriptstyle 1 \end{array}$

$3 \times 2 = 6$
$6 + 1$ gives 7

---

2 Work these out.

a $\begin{array}{r} 16 \\ \times 2 \\ \hline \\ \hline \end{array}$
b $\begin{array}{r} 15 \\ \times 3 \\ \hline \\ \hline \end{array}$
c $\begin{array}{r} 24 \\ \times 5 \\ \hline \\ \hline \end{array}$
d $\begin{array}{r} 34 \\ \times 4 \\ \hline \\ \hline \end{array}$
e $\begin{array}{r} 47 \\ \times 2 \\ \hline \\ \hline \end{array}$

3 Set these out in the same way. Then work them out.

a 25×3 **b** 33×5 **c** 48×4 **d** 46×5

Bigger numbers can be worked out in the same way.

Example 164×2

```
  H  T  U
  1  6  4
×        2
─────────
  3  2  8
  1
```

$2 \times 4 = 8$ **8** goes in the units column.
$2 \times 6 = 12$ **2** goes in the tens column and **1** to carry.
$2 \times 1 = 2$ Add the **1** from the carry to make **3** which goes in the hundreds column.

Work these out.

4 **a** 163
          $\times 3$
          ─────
          ─────

   c 142
          $\times 4$
          ─────
          ─────

   e 231
          $\times 5$
          ─────
          ─────

   g 156
          $\times 2$
          ─────
          ─────

   b 152
          $\times 3$
          ─────
          ─────

   d 308
          $\times 2$
          ─────
          ─────

   f 314
          $\times 5$
          ─────
          ─────

   h 433
          $\times 4$
          ─────
          ─────

To multiply by a number ending in 0, write the 0 in the units column then multiply by the number.

Examples 36×20 23×50

```
        36                23
     ×  20             ×  50
     ─────             ─────
       720              1150
```

5 **a** 24×20 **c** 35×40 **e** 52×30
   b 24×30 **d** 41×50 **f** 35×50

Here is one way to multiply 2 large numbers.
You can do it in stages.

Example 23×15

First do 23×5 Then do 23×10 Now add the two answers together.

```
      23                23                115
   ×   5             ×  10             + 230
   ─────             ─────             ─────
     115               230               345
```

$$23 \times 15 = 345$$

6 **a** 24×14 **c** 45×13 **e** 31×13
   b 32×12 **d** 22×15 **f** 54×14

Division

These all mean the same:

How many times does 3 go into 69?

How many 3s are there in 69?

Divide 69 by 3

$69 \div 3 = 23$ First divide 6 by 3 $6 \div 3 = 2$ $\dfrac{23}{3\overline{)69}}$
Then divide 9 by 3 $9 \div 3 = 3$

Exercise 2:9

1 **a** $2\overline{)46}$ **b** $3\overline{)93}$ **c** $5\overline{)550}$ **d** $4\overline{)84}$

Sometimes you have to 'carry'.

Example $96 \div 4$ $4\overline{)96}$

First do 9 divided by 4. This is 2 with 1 left over.

$\dfrac{2}{4\overline{)9^16}}$ Write it like this.
      Put the **2** over the **9** and carry the **1**.

$\dfrac{2\,4}{4\overline{)9^16}}$ Now do 16 divided by 4. This is 4.
      Put the **4** over the **6**, like this.

Work these out. You can write them another way.

2 **a** $2\overline{)36}$ **d** $2\overline{)78}$ **g** $80 \div 5$
   b $3\overline{)57}$ **e** $3\overline{)78}$ **h** $158 \div 2$
   c $5\overline{)65}$ **f** $4\overline{)132}$ **i** $411 \div 3$

2

Sometimes there is a remainder left at the end.

Example $37 \div 2$

$$\begin{array}{r} 1\,8 \\ 2\overline{)3^17} \end{array} \quad \text{remainder } \mathbf{1}$$
$\qquad\qquad\qquad (17 \div 2 = 8 \quad \text{remainder } 1)$

These divisions have remainders.
Work out the divisions.

3 **a** $33 \div 2$ **c** $221 \div 2$ **e** $36 \div 5$ **g** $74 \div 4$

      b $46 \div 3$ **d** $142 \div 3$ **f** $54 \div 4$

Target Ten

1 Gemma has 50 p. She buys a torch at 28 p. How much change does she receive?

2 Matthew buys a belt for 65 p. He gives the shopkeeper £1. How much change does he get?

3 Mike buys four batteries at £1.10 each. How much does he spend?

4 If lollipops are 6 p each, how many can Abi buy with 20 p?

5 Share £24 equally between 4 girls. How much will each get?

6 A box of 6 eggs costs 36 p. How much is one egg?

7 Mrs Cook shares 13 chocolate eggs equally between her four children. How many does each receive? How many are left for Mrs Cook?

8 Four friends buy old comics from Charlene, each paying her 25 p. How much money does Charlene get?

9 Louise has 19 sweets to share equally between 6 friends. How many will each friend receive? How many are left over?

10 Stuart spends 16 p, then 24 p. How much change does he have left from £1?

1 Copy each pair of checkout slips below. For each pair:
   (1) Find the *TOTAL* of the first slip by adding.
   (2) Find the *TOTAL* of the second slip by multiplying.
   (3) Check that the *TOTALS* are the same.

a

ICE CREAM	32 p
ICE CREAM	32 p
ICE CREAM	32 p
ICE CREAM	32 p
TOTAL	......

b

CRISPS	12 p
CRISPS	12 p
CRISPS	12 p
TOTAL	......

c

FRUIT BAR	40 P
FRUIT BAR	40 P
FRUIT BAR	40 P
FRUIT BAR	40 P
FRUIT BAR	40 P
TOTAL	......

ICE CREAMS	TOTAL
...... @ 32 p	......

CRISPS	TOTAL
...... @ 12 p	......

FRUIT BARS	TOTAL
...... @ 40 p	......

2 Write these additions as multiplications.

   a 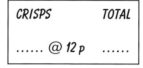 +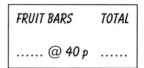

   b $6 + 6 + 6 + 6$

   c $8 + 8 + 8 + 8 + 8$

   d $2 + 2 + 2 + 2 + 2 + 2 + 2$

3 Linda has 20 soaps.
   She keeps them in boxes of 4.
   She fills the boxes like this.

1st box	$20 - 4 = 16$ soaps left
2nd box	$16 - 4 = \ldots$ soaps left
3rd box	$\ldots - \ldots = \ldots$ soaps left
... box	$\ldots - \ldots = \ldots$ soaps left
... box	$\ldots - \ldots = 0$ soaps left

   a Copy and complete the table.

   b How many times does Linda take away 4?

   c How many boxes does she fill?

   d Check your answer with this division $20 \div 4 = \ldots$

4 Jay has 33 sunflower seeds.
He plants them in rows of 6 seeds.

   a How many rows can he fill?

   b How many seeds will be left over?

5 What is the change from 20p when I spend:

   a 16p   **b** 11p   **c** 8p   **d** 18p   **e** 6p

6 What is the change from £1 when I spend:

   a 75p   **b** 55p   **c** 66p   **d** 44p   **e** 19p

7 What is the change from £5 when I spend:

   a £2.75   **b** £1.55   **c** £3.66   **d** £4.44   **e** £2.19

8

a	**b**	**c**	**d**	**e**
42	19	35	26	34
$\times 4$	$\times 2$	$\times 5$	$\times 20$	$\times 14$

9 **a** $3\overline{)69}$ **b** $75 \div 5$ **c** $3\overline{)156}$ **d** $240 \div 4$

10 **a** $3\overline{)71}$ **b** $78 \div 5$ **c** $39 \div 4$ **d** $2\overline{)127}$

3 Symmetry

QUESTIONS

The photograph on the left shows Peter's face.

The photograph on the right shows what happens if the left half of Peter's face is reflected in a mirror line.

What are the differences between the two photographs?

1 Line symmetry

Exercise 3:1

1 **a** Fold a piece of paper in half.

b Draw a design on one side of your paper like this:
It must start and finish on the fold.

c Cut along your design with scissors.

d Open out the paper.

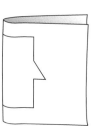

e Draw a dotted line along the fold.

f Put a mirror along the dotted line.
Look at the reflection in the mirror.
Look at the part of your design that
is behind the mirror.
They are the same.

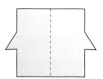

2 Use two more pieces of paper.
Fold each piece in half.
Follow the instructions above to get two more shapes.

3 Stick your three pieces of paper in your book.

| **Image** | The **image** is what we see in the mirror. |

| **Line of symmetry** | The fold is called the **line of symmetry** or mirror line. |

A line of symmetry divides a shape into two equal parts.
If you fold the shape along this line, each part fits exactly on top of the other.
The line of symmetry is shown as a dotted line.

4 a Fold a piece of paper in half.
Fold it in half again.

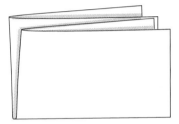

b Draw a design on your paper like this:
It must start and finish on the folded sides.

c Cut along your design with scissors.

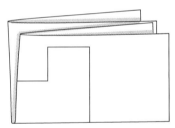

d Open out the paper.

e Draw a dotted line along both of the folds.

f Put a mirror along one dotted line.
Look at the image in the mirror.
Do the same for the other fold.

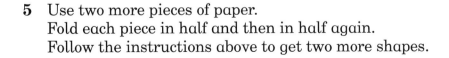

g How many lines of symmetry does the shape have?

5 Use two more pieces of paper.
Fold each piece in half and then in half again.
Follow the instructions above to get two more shapes.

6 Stick your three pieces of paper in your book.

Example **a** How many sides does this
shape have?
b How many lines of symmetry
does this shape have?
Use folding to find out.

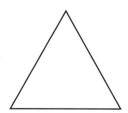

a The shape has 3 sides.
b Fold the shape in half, so that each part fits exactly on top of the
other, as many different ways as possible.
Draw dotted lines along the folds.

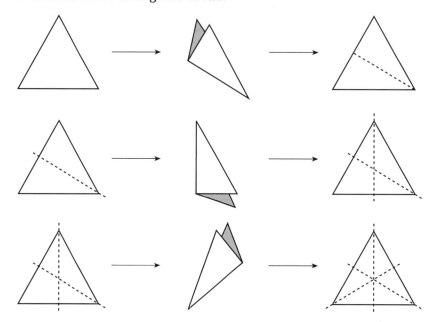

The shape has 3 lines of symmetry.
This can be checked by putting a mirror on each line of symmetry.

W 1   **7** Cut out the equilateral triangle from the worksheet.
Fold the triangle to find all the lines of symmetry.
Mark the lines of symmetry with dotted lines.
Check using a mirror.

W 1, 2   **8** **a** Cut out each shape on the worksheet.
b Fold each shape to find all the lines of symmetry.
Mark them with dotted lines.
Check using a mirror.
c Fill in the number of sides and the number of lines of
symmetry in the table on the worksheet.
G 1   **d** Stick your shapes and your table into your book.
Write the name of the shape underneath each one.

The word **regular** means that all the sides of the shape are the same length.

9 Which shape on the worksheet is not regular?

10 Look at your table.
Copy and complete:
'For the regular shapes, I noticed that the number of sides and the number of lines of symmetry were …'

Example How many lines of symmetry does this shape have?
Use tracing paper to find out.
Mark the lines of symmetry with a dotted line.

Trace the shape onto tracing paper.

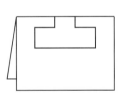

Fold the tracing paper to find the lines of symmetry.
Mark the lines of symmetry on the first shape.
This shape has two lines of symmetry.

Exercise 3:2

1 a Copy these shapes onto squared paper. Trace each one.
b Fold the tracing paper to find all the lines of symmetry.
c Mark the lines of symmetry on the shapes on the squared paper.

1

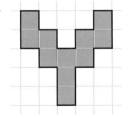

2

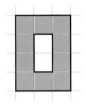

3

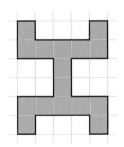

Example   Any point can be reflected in a line of symmetry.

The image is on the other side of the line of symmetry.
The image is the same distance away from the line of symmetry as
the object.
A line joining the image and the object is at right angles to the line
of symmetry.

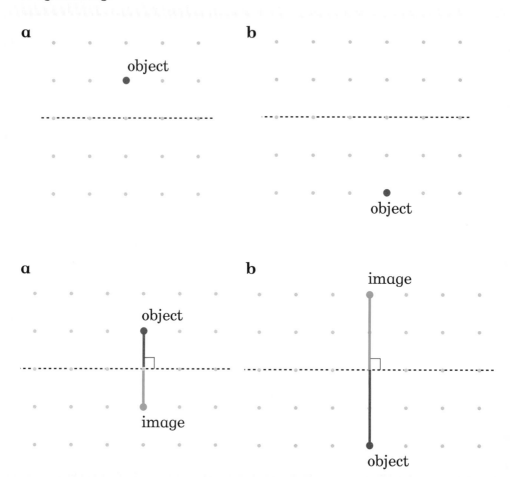

Check using a mirror or a piece of tracing paper.

Exercise 3:3

You will need a worksheet.

 1 Reflect these points in the lines of symmetry.
Check using a mirror or tracing paper.

Example   You can only see half of this shape.
Use the line of symmetry to complete the shape.

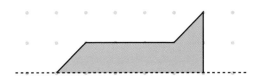

Each point on the image must be the same distance
from the line of symmetry but on the other side.
Choose some points on the original object and then
mark the same points after they have been reflected.
Join the points to get the reflection.

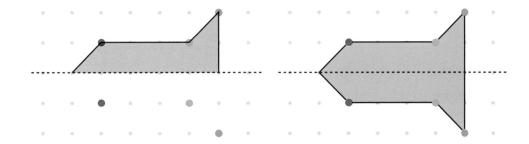

Place a mirror along the line of symmetry to check the answer.

2 Copy each shape onto squared dotty paper.
Use the line of symmetry to complete the shape.
Use a mirror to check your answers.

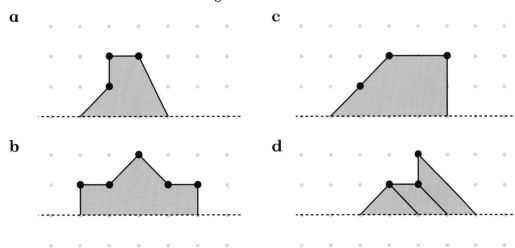

3 **3** Copy each shape onto squared dotty paper.
Use the line of symmetry to complete the shape.

a 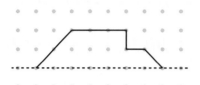 **b**

4 **4** Copy these patterns onto squared dotty paper.
Use the line of symmetry to complete the pattern.

a 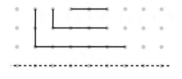 **b**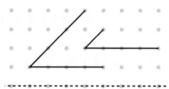

Example

This is a pattern of shaded squares.
The dotted line **should be** a line of
symmetry but two squares are missing.

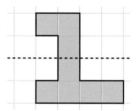

Louise shades in two more squares.
Now the dotted line **is** a line of symmetry.

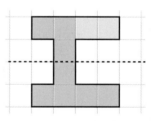

Exercise 3:4

5 **1** Copy these shapes onto squared paper.
Shade in one more square to make the line of symmetry correct.

a 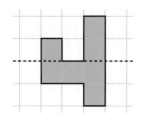 **b**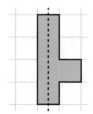

2 Copy these shapes onto squared paper.
Shade in two more squares to make the line of symmetry correct.

a

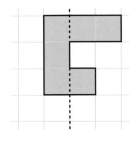

c

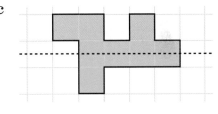

b

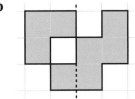

d

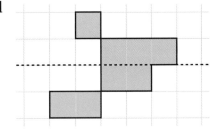

A mirror line can be at an angle.
The image is still the same distance from the line of symmetry as the object.
The line joining the image and the object is still at right angles to the line of symmetry.

Example
Reflect this point in the line of symmetry.

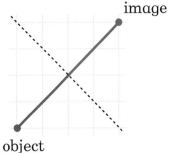

W4 **3** Reflect these points in the lines of symmetry.
Check using a mirror or tracing paper.

6 **4** Copy these shapes onto squared paper.
Use the line of symmetry to complete the shapes.
Use a mirror to check the answer.

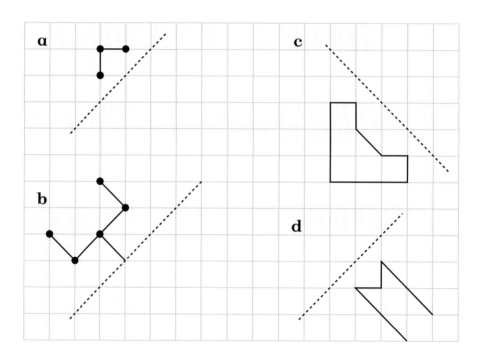

5 Copy these shapes onto squared paper.
Use the line of symmetry to complete the shapes.
Use a mirror to check the answer.

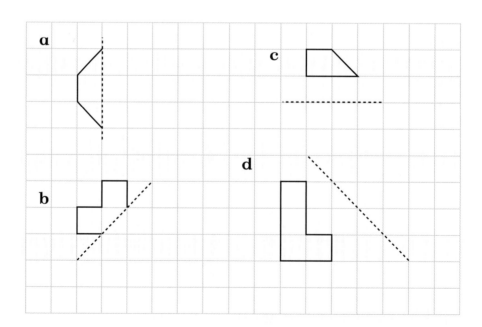

2 Rotational symmetry

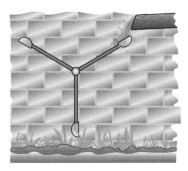

This is a pelton wheel.
It moves water by turning.
From the side it looks the same as it turns.

Rotation	A **rotation** is a turning movement round in a circle.
Rotational symmetry	A shape has **rotational symmetry** if it fits on top of itself more than once as it makes a complete turn.
Order of rotational symmetry	The **order of rotational symmetry** is the number of times that the shape fits on top of itself as it makes one complete turn. This must be 2 or more.

Lydia sketches this shape onto tracing paper.
She marks the centre with a dot.
This is the **centre** of rotational symmetry.
She marks a cross on one point of the shape.

Lydia rotates the paper over the picture. She counts the number of times it fits exactly on top of itself until the cross returns to where it started.

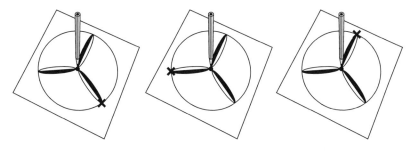

This shape has rotational symmetry of order 3.

Exercise 3:5

 7

For each shape:

a Trace the shape. Mark a cross on one point of the shape.
The centre of rotation is marked as a dot.

b Use the tracing paper to see how many times the shape fits
on top of itself in one complete turn.

c Write down the order of rotational symmetry.
If a shape has no rotational symmetry, write 'none'.

1
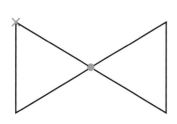

4
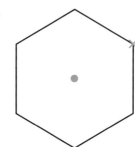

2
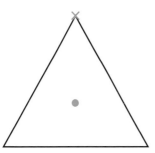

5
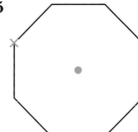

3
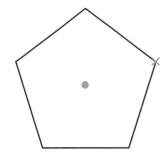

6
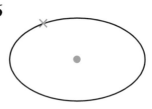

 3

3 Symmetry in 3-D

David has made some solids with cubes.
All the shapes are symmetrical in 3-D.
He has drawn the solids on isometric paper.

Isometric paper is printed in triangles.

It has a right way up.

right ✓   wrong ✗

Exercise 3:6

You will need isometric paper and Multilink cubes for this exercise.

1 Make sure your paper is the right way up.

2 (1) Make each of the solids below using Multilink.
  (2) Copy each of the diagrams onto isometric paper.

a   b   c

3 a Make this arrangement of cubes.

b Put the arrangement in front of you
on the desk.

c Copy the picture onto isometric paper.
Make sure that the paper is the right
way up.

4 (1) Make each of the solids below.
(2) Put the arrangements in front of you on the desk.
(3) Draw each of the arrangements of cubes on isometric paper.

a

d

b

e

c

f

This solid is symmetrical on both sides of the mirror.

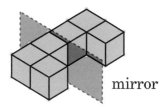

mirror

Example   Complete this solid so that it is symmetrical on both sides of the mirror.

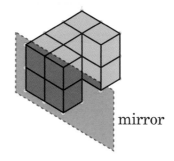

mirror

The completed solid looks like this:

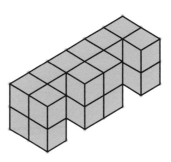

Exercise 3:7

Make each of these solids with cubes.
Complete each solid so that it is symmetrical on both sides of the mirror.
Draw the complete solid on dotty isometric paper.

1 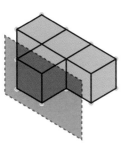   **2** 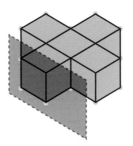   **3**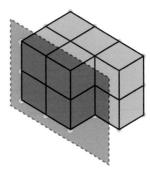

1 Copy each shape onto squared paper.
Mark all the lines of symmetry on each shape.
You can use tracing paper to help you.

a
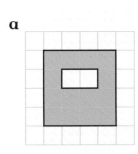

b
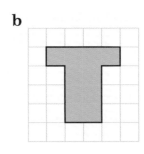

c
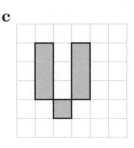

2 Copy each shape onto squared dotty paper.
Use the line of symmetry to complete the shape.

a
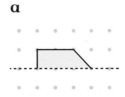

b

c
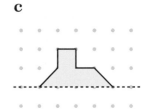

3 Copy each shape onto squared paper.
Use the line of symmetry to complete the shape.

a   b   c
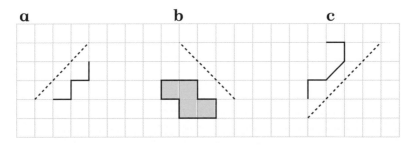

4 For each shape:
(1) Trace the shape. Mark a cross on one point of the shape.
(2) Use tracing paper to see how many times the shape fits on
top of itself in one complete turn.
(3) Write down the order of rotational symmetry.

a

b
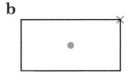

c

4 Statistics

QUESTIONS

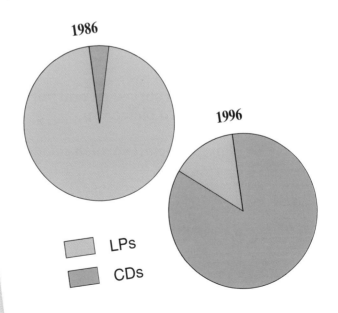

Relative share of retail sales in UK held by LPs and CDs (albums only) in 1986 and 1996.

1986

1996

LPs

CDs

Source: unpublished data.

1 Pictograms and bar-charts

The results of surveys can be shown as diagrams.

| **Pictogram** | A **pictogram** is a diagram that uses *all* or *part* of the same picture each time. The pictures must line up in columns. |

| **Key** | There must be a **key** to show what each picture represents. |

Example

   ♀   represents 2 children

   ↯   represents 1 child

 ♀♀↯   represents 2 + 2 + 1 = 5 children

Exercise 4:1

1 Mya has done a survey on nail varnish.
   She has drawn a pictogram.

   Favourite nail varnish colour

   Clear   ◖◗ ◖◗   *Key:*
   Pink   ◖◗ ◖   ◖◗ represents
   Red   2 people
   Rainbow ◖◗ ◖◗ ◖◗ ◖◗ ◖

   a How many chose **i** clear **ii** pink **iii** rainbow?

   b Five people chose red nail varnish.
   In your exercise book draw the line for red nail varnish.

2 Marcos has done a survey on ice cream flavours.
He has put his results in a table.

Flavour	Vanilla	Strawberry	Chocolate	Banana
Number of pupils	8	5	6	3

Marcos draws a pictogram.

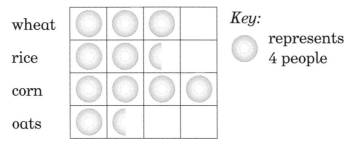

Favourite ice cream flavours

Vanilla

Strawberry

Chocolate

Banana

Key:

represents 2 people

In your exercise book draw the line for **a** chocolate **b** banana.

3 Joe did his survey on favourite breakfast cereals.
Here is his pictogram.

Favourite breakfast cereal

wheat

rice

corn

oats

Key:

represents 4 people

a How many chose (1) wheat (2) rice (3) corn (4) oats.

b How many people did Joe ask altogether?

You may have to *estimate* the number represented by the picture in a pictogram.

Example   (☺) represents 10 people.

How many people are represented by (☺ ?

(☺ is more than half.

An estimate is 7 people.

4   (☺) represents 10 people.

Estimate the number of people represented by:

a (☺   b (☺)   c (

5    ▲ represents 5 ice lollies.

Estimate the number of ice lollies represented by:

a ▲   b /   c ▲

6    ✉ represents 10 envelopes.

a Estimate the number of envelopes represented by:

(1) 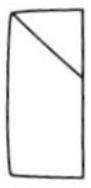 ▯   (2)  ✉   (3)  |

b Draw a picture to represent
   (1) 5 envelopes   (2) 9 envelopes.

7 Some pupils in Year 9 belong to sports clubs.
Adam is drawing a pictogram to show this.

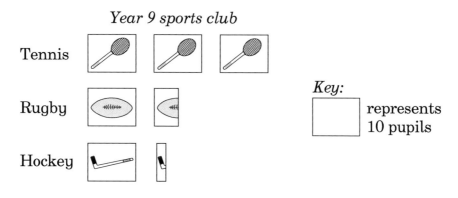

Year 9 sports club

Tennis

Rugby

Key:

represents
10 pupils

Hockey

Football

a How many belong to the tennis club?

b Estimate the number in the rugby club.

c Estimate the number in the hockey club.

d 35 pupils belong to the football club.
Draw pictures for the football line in your exercise book.

8 Year 9 had a day out.
The pictogram shows where they went.

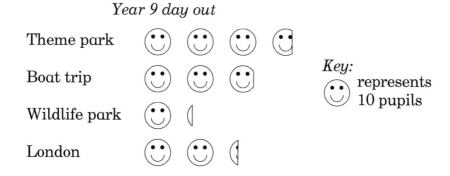

Year 9 day out

Theme park

Boat trip

Key:

represents
10 pupils

Wildlife park

London

Answer **true** or **false** to each statement.

a About 30 pupils went to the theme park.

b About 29 pupils went on a boat trip.

c About 15 pupils went to the wildlife park.

d About 25 pupils went to London.

e Altogether about 100 pupils had a day out.

Exercise 4:2

1 Paula has collected data on the number of hours her friends spend on the computer in one week.
She has drawn a bar-chart to show her data.

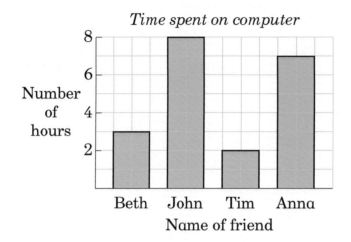

a Beth spent 3 hours on her computer.
How many hours did Anna spend on her computer?

b How many hours did John spend on his computer?

c Who spent the least time on their computer?

2 This bar-chart shows the time each member of the Williams family spends getting to work or school.

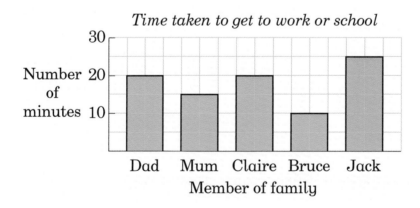

a Jack took 25 minutes to travel to work.
How long did Claire take to travel to school?

b Claire and Bruce both walk to school at the same speed.
Whose school is nearest to their house?

c How long did Mum take to travel to work?

3   The table shows how many holidays different families take.

Number of holidays	Number of families
0	4
1	12
2	7
3	2
4	1

Kari draws a bar-chart to show the data.
Use the table to complete the chart.

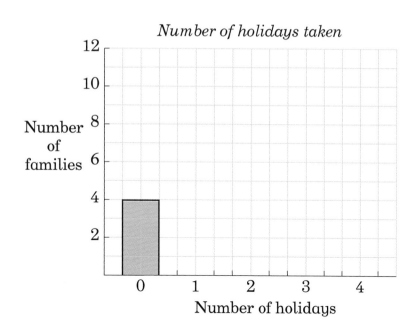

a How many families have (1)   no holiday?

(2)   1 holiday?

(3)   **more** than 1 holiday?

(4)   2 holidays?

(5)   **less** than 2 holidays?

b How many families are there altogether?

4 These bar-charts are for two families.
They show how the families spent money one weekend.

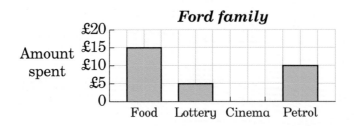

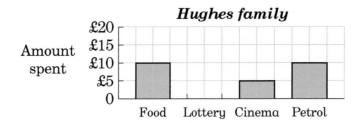

a Which family did not buy lottery tickets?
b Which family spent most money on food?
c How much did the Hughes family spend at the cinema?
d How much did the Hughes family spend altogether?
e How much did the Ford family spend altogether?
f Which family spent the most money?
g How much more did they spend?

5 Neave earns £18 a week working in a shop.
This is how she spent the money last week:

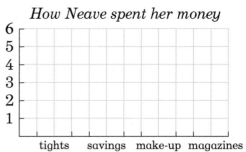

Draw a bar-chart using Neave's data.

2 Tally-tables and groups

Peter and Jane are doing a survey.

They are asking pupils to choose their next school trip.

They record the data in a tally-table.

Tally-marks **Tally-marks** are done in groups of five. The fifth tally-mark goes across the other four: This makes them easier to count.

Example

Tally	Total
				3
ﷻ		6

Exercise 4:3

1 Here are the results of Peter and Jane's survey.
They asked where pupils would choose to go.

School trip	Tally	Total
canal	ﷻ ﷻ ﷻ	
mountain	ﷻ ﷻ |||	
city	ﷻ ﷻ ﷻ ﷻ		
seaside	ﷻ ﷻ ﷻ ||||	

a Write down the total for:
(1) canal (2) mountain (3) city (4) seaside
b How many pupils did Peter and Jane ask altogether?

Frequency   **Frequency** means the number of times something happens.

---

2 Ann has done a survey on the number of times people go out in one month. She asked 20 people. This is her data:

⓪ ① ③ ① ① ② ① ④ ⓪ ②
1   2   0   1   3   0   1   2   1   2

W 1

Complete the tally-table below. The circled numbers have been entered already.

Number of times	Tally	Frequency
0	||	
1	||||	
2	||	
3	|	
4	|	

W 2 **3** Derek wants to find out which colour ink his friends like to use. Here is his data.

~~black~~	~~black~~	~~blue~~	~~black~~	blue	green
~~blue~~	~~green~~	~~black~~	red	black	blue
~~black~~	~~blue~~	~~black~~	black	black	black

a Copy and complete the tally-table below. The data that are crossed out have already been put in.

Colour of ink	Tally	Frequency
green	|	
black	卌 |	
blue	|||	
red		

b Draw a pictogram to show Derek's data. Choose a symbol to represent **two** friends.

Survey

Conduct your own survey on 'hair colour' for pupils in your class.
Fill in the tally-table.

Hair colour	Tally	Total
fair		
medium brown		
very dark		
redhead		

Draw a pictogram to show your results.

Hair colour

Key:
 represents 2 pupils

fair	
medium brown	
very dark	
redhead	

 Survey

Conduct a survey of your own.
Choose any subject you like (e.g. chocolate bars, crisps, cars, sportswear names, etc.).
Select 4 or 5 items to choose from.
Draw a tally-table, listing your choices.
Ask up to 30 people to choose.

Pictogram   Draw a symbol.
Write down the key.
Show your results in a pictogram.

or
Bar-chart   Draw a bar-chart.
Remember to label your axes clearly.

Grouped data

Example   Here are the marks the pupils in 9R scored in a test.
The marks are out of 30.

15	4	7	28	17	3	29	21
17	4	19	26	7	27	11	5
8	18	12	6	24	15	19	26

a Make a tally-table of the data.
b Draw a bar-chart.

a A tally-table showing every mark separately would be too long.
This sort of data needs to be in groups,
e.g. all numbers 1 to 10 go in the first group 1–10.

Time (min)	Tally	Frequency
1–10	ЖЖ |||	8
11–20	ЖЖ ЖЖ	10
21–30	ЖЖ		6

b When you use
grouped data the
bars must touch.

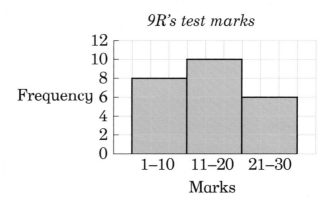

9R's test marks

---

4 Mr Gray marked his class's maths homework.
Here are the marks they received out of 59.

(18) (52) (43) (42) 49 13 26 28

(38) (30) (36) (19) 28 36 54 18

(51) (59) (28) (51) 14 29 21 16

Copy and complete the tally-table on the next page.

Marks	Tally	Frequency
0–19	||	
20–39	||||	
40–59	ⅢⅠ |	

5 Finn's data shows how many minutes trains were late due to track work.

4   20   17   12   19   17   16   10
16   18   9   20   2   15   19   12
13   7   16   16   11   20   6   20

a Copy and complete the tally-table.

Minutes late	Tally	Total
1–5	|	
6–10	||	
11–15	||	
16–20	ⅢⅠ ||	

b How many trains were 6–10 minutes late?

c How many trains altogether were 10 minutes late or less?

d By how long were most trains late?

e How many train times were checked?

f Copy these axes.
Draw a bar-chart.

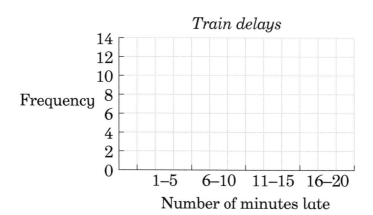

Train delays

Frequency (vertical axis: 0, 2, 4, 6, 8, 10, 12, 14)

Number of minutes late (horizontal axis: 1–5, 6–10, 11–15, 16–20)

Example   The bar-chart shows the time taken by pupils in 9S to travel to school.

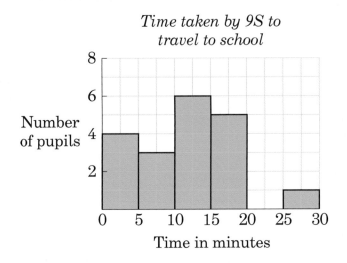

Time taken by 9S to travel to school

a How many pupils took less than 10 minutes to travel to school?

We need all the pupils in the 0–5 and 5–10 groups.
Answer: 4 + 3 = 7 pupils

b How many pupils took more than 15 minutes to travel to school?

We need all the pupils in the 15–20, 20–25 and 25–30 groups.
Answer: 5 + 0 + 1 = 6 pupils

6   Terry's bar-chart shows the height of some seedlings.
Terry measured the plants two months after the seeds were sown.

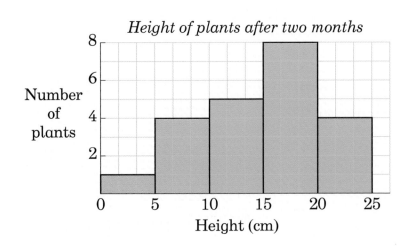

Height of plants after two months

a How many plants are less than 5 cm?

b How many plants are between 5 cm and 10 cm?

c How many plants altogether are less than 10 cm?

d Which group of heights was the most common?

e How many plants are more than 20 cm high?

f How many plants altogether are more than 15 cm high?

g What was the total number of seedlings planted?

7 Ann organised a quiz. The scores were out of 20. The tally-table shows the scores of 16 people who took part.

Number of marks	Tally	Total
1–5	||	
6–10	|||	
11–15	ⅲ|| ||	
16–20	||||	

a Copy the tally-table. Fill in the Total column.

b Copy these axes. Draw a bar-chart to show the results.

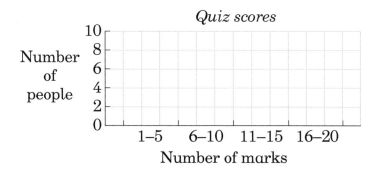

Quiz scores

Number of people

Number of marks

Activity

- In your group, for each person count the number of letters in their first name *and* surname.
- Put your results in a tally-table using groups 1–5, 6–10, etc.
- Draw a bar-chart to show your results.
- What does your bar-chart tell you?

3 Pie-charts

How Michael spent 24 hours

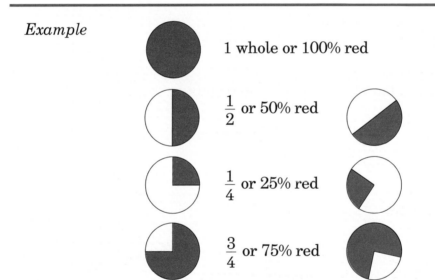

Example

1 whole or 100% red

$\frac{1}{2}$ or 50% red

$\frac{1}{4}$ or 25% red

$\frac{3}{4}$ or 75% red

Exercise 4:4

1 **a** Cut out the circle.
   b Fold the circle in half.
   c Fold the circle again into quarters.
   d Open up the circle.
   e Colour half the circle red.
   f Colour a quarter of the circle blue.
   g Colour the other quarter yellow.
   h Stick the circle into your exercise book.

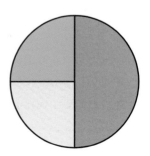

2 The whole circle is 100%.

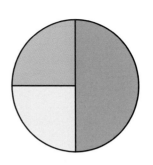

a What fraction is red?

b What is half of 100%?

c What percentage of the circle is red?

d What is one quarter of 100%?

e What percentage is blue?

f What percentage is yellow?

3

(A)　　　　(B)　　　　(C)　　　　(D)　　　　(E)　　　　(F)

Look at the diagrams above.

Write down the letters for the ones that are:

a more than 50% blue

b less than 25% blue

c more than 25% but less than 50% blue.

Sometimes we can only 'estimate' the percentage.

W 6

Activity – 'Matching Percentages'

Example 　Look at the pie-chart.

a Estimate the percentage that buy lunch in the canteen (red).

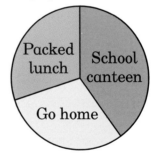

What pupils do for lunch

Answer: The red slice is under half.
It is less than 50%.
Estimate: 40%
(Any answer between 37% and 45% would be correct.)

b Estimate the percentage that bring a packed lunch (blue).

Answer: The blue slice is a bit more than a quarter.
It is a bit more than 25%.
Estimate: 28%
(Any answer between 26% and 32% would be correct.)

7 4 Estimate the percentage that is coloured red in each of these pie-charts.
Stick the worksheet into your exercise book.

a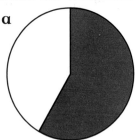

Red is just over … %
Estimate … %

c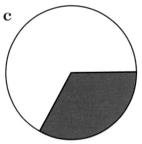

Red is just over … %
Estimate … %

b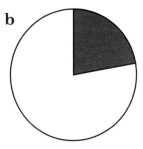

Red is just under … %
Estimate … %

d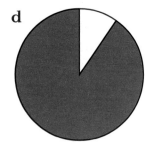

Red is just under … %
Estimate … %

 8 5 Shade in the amount shown as near as you can.

a

30% red

c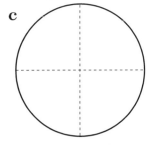

90 % blue

b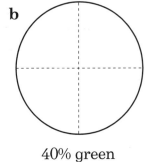

40% green

d

10% yellow

6 These pie-charts show how pupils in different years feel about school uniform.

Year 7   Year 9   Year 11

a Which year has about 20% who like uniform?
b Which year has about 60% who like uniform?
c Which year has the largest percentage of pupils who like wearing uniform?
  This section is just over 75%.
  Estimate the percentage for this year.

- -

It is usually easier to estimate the smaller percentages.
We can then find the larger percentages by subtracting from 100%.

Example

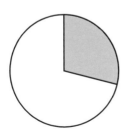

The pink section is about 30%.

So the yellow section is about
  100% − 30% = 70%

Check: 30% + 70% = 100%

Exercise 4:5

1 For each pie-chart:
  (1) estimate as a percentage the smaller section
  (2) estimate the other section by subtracting from 100%
  (3) check that your two answers add up to 100%.

a **b** **c** **d**

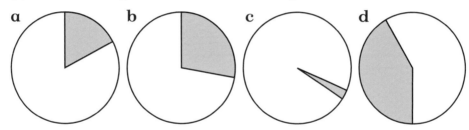

4

2 The pie-chart shows how the Earth's surface is divided into land and water.
From the pie-chart,

   a estimate the percentage of land

   b estimate the percentage of water by subtracting from 100%.

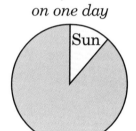

The Earth's surface

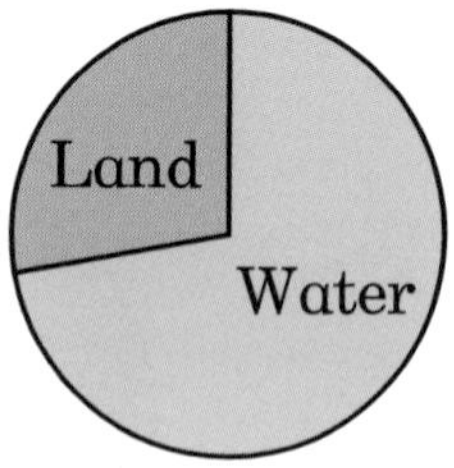

3 The pie-chart shows the number of hours of sunshine on a day in January.

   a Estimate the percentage of the day when the Sun was shining.

   b Estimate the percentage of the day when the Sun was **not** shining.

Hours of sunshine on one day

4 The pie-chart shows what cornflakes contain.

   a What percentage is carbohydrate?

   b Estimate the percentage that is protein?

   c Estimate the percentage that is fat. (Subtract the answers to **a** and **b** from 100%.)

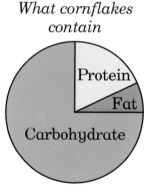

What cornflakes contain

G 3, 4

Activity – My school day

1 Use the worksheets to collect data about your day.

W 9, 10   2 Use the data to draw a pie-chart.

3 Use the pie-chart to estimate percentages.

8

1 Lisa has asked 20 of her friends which flavour of crisps they liked best out of:

The pictogram shows the results.

plain

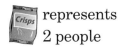 represents 2 people

salt and vinegar

cheese and onion

How many of Lisa's friends chose:

a salt and vinegar crisps

b cheese and onion crisps?

2 ⚽ represents 12 people.

Estimate the number of people represented by:

a 　　**b** 　　**c** ⚽

3 Steve asked 20 people which running event they liked the best.
The results are shown in the table.
Draw a bar-chart to show this data.

Event	Number of people
100 metres	6
400 metres	3
800 metres	9
1500 metres	2

4   The bar-chart below shows 'Favourite field events.'

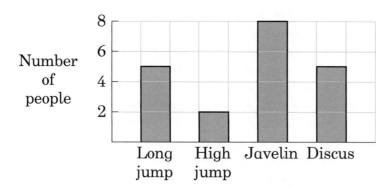

a   How many chose javelin?

b   How many chose long jump?

c   How many were in the group altogether?

W 11

5   Ray has done a survey on the number of times people go to the supermarket in a week.
He asked 20 people.
This is his data:

② ⑤ ①   4   2

③ ④ ②   1   1

⑤ ⑦   3   3   2

② ③   2   5   2

a Copy and complete the tally-table below.
The first 10 numbers have already been put in.

Number of times	Tally	Frequency
1		
2					
3				
4			
5				
6		
7			

b Draw a pictogram to show Ray's data.

Use the key  to represent 2 visits.

W 12 **6** Here are the times 20 pupils in 9S take to get ready in the morning.
The times are in minutes.

⑤	⑮	㉚	45	12
⑧	⑳	(60)	35	25
㉚	㊵	25	50	20
⑩	㉕	55	15	70

Time (min)	Tally	Frequency
1–20	卌	
21–40	||||	
41–60	|	
61–80		

On the worksheet,

a Complete the tally-table – the first 10 numbers have been put in already.

b Draw a bar-chart for the grouped data.

c How many pupils took 40 minutes or less to get ready?

d How many pupils took over an hour to get ready?

13   **7** Shade the following amounts on the pie-charts.

a 100%

b 50%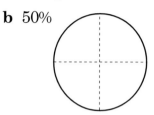

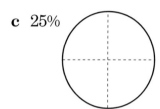

c 25%

d 75%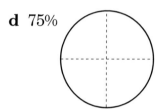

13   **8** Estimate the percentage shaded in each of the pie-charts by completing the following:

a

Shaded part is just over ... %

Estimate   ... %

b

Shaded part is just under   ... %

Estimate   ... %

9 On the pie-charts, shade in the amount shown as near as you can.

a 40%   **b** 90%   **c** 60%

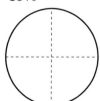   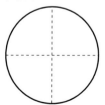   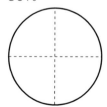

5 Estimation and measurement

Imagine you could drop Mount Everest into the
Mariana Trench in the Pacific Ocean.

How many kilometres of water would there be
above the top of the mountain?

1 Estimation

Example   How old was baby George when he first smiled at Mum?

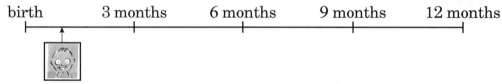

Estimate: Baby George was about one month old when he first smiled.

Exercise 5:1

1 a How old was George when he first sat up?

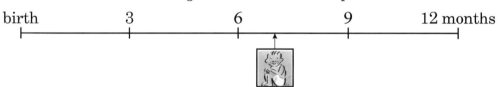

b How old was George when he said his first words?

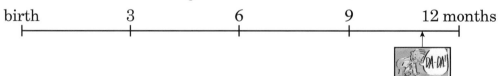

c How old was George when he started to walk?

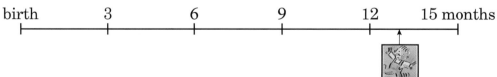

George's older sister is called Alice.

Example   The picture shows Alice starting school.

    a Put the picture in the correct box on the time line.

    b Estimate Alice's age and write it in the space.

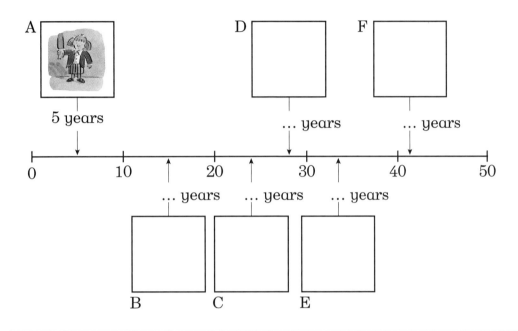

A   D   F

5 years   ... years   ... years

0   10   20   30   40   50

... years   ... years   ... years

B   C   E

W1

2 These pictures show Alice when she is older.

Buying a house   Running a marathon   Getting engaged   Having a baby   Leaving school

    a Cut out the pictures.

    b Arrange them in the order you think Alice would do them.

    c Stick the pictures into the boxes in the order you choose.

    d Using the time line estimate Alice's age for each picture and write your estimate in the space provided.

3 Estimate the dates of the events marked on the time line below.

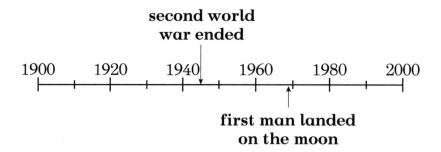

second world
war ended

1900   1920   1940   1960   1980   2000

first man landed
on the moon

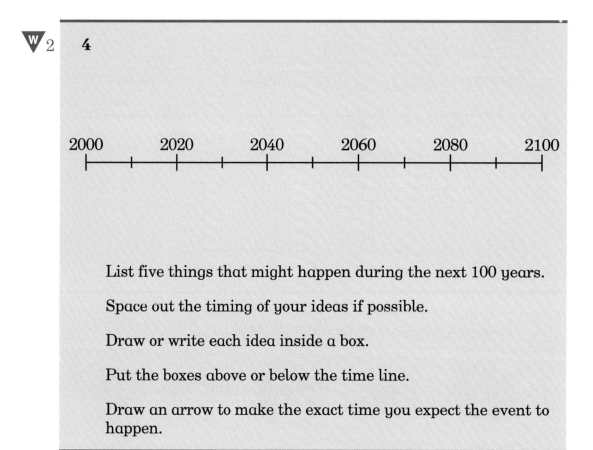

4

2000   2020   2040   2060   2080   2100

List five things that might happen during the next 100 years.

Space out the timing of your ideas if possible.

Draw or write each idea inside a box.

Put the boxes above or below the time line.

Draw an arrow to make the exact time you expect the event to happen.

Estimating lengths

You can estimate lengths using the following units:
millimetres (**mm**)
centimetres (**cm**)
metres (**m**)
kilometres (**km**)

Example   What units would you use to measure:

Answer

a a pin?   **mm**

b a large envelope?   **cm**

c a house?   **m**

d a car rally route?   **km**

Exercise 5:2

1   Write the correct units for these measurements.
Choose from **mm**, **cm**, **m** or **km**.

a

Length of a
paper clip
20 ...

c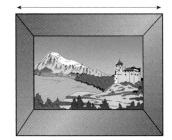

The picture is 30 ... across

b

Height of a
lamp post 5 ...

d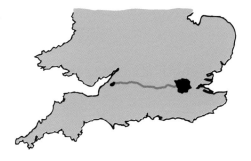

Bristol to London 170 ...

W 3 **2** Match the estimates to the correct picture.
The first one has been done for you.

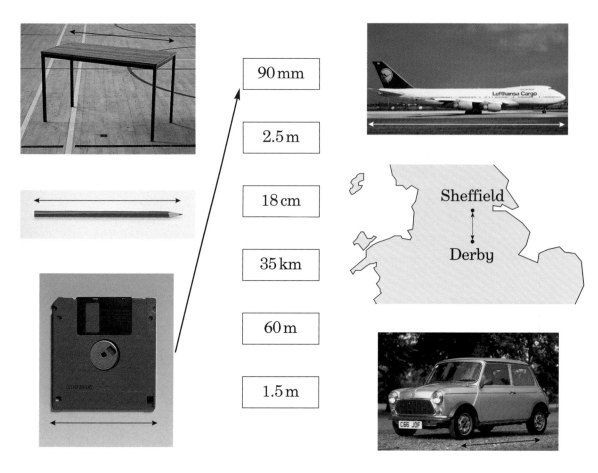

90 mm

2.5 m

18 cm

35 km

60 m

1.5 m

Choose the correct answer and write it down.

3 The length of a swimming pool could be:
a 25 cm
b 25 m
c 25 km

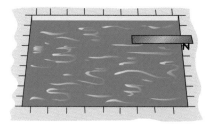

4 The length of an eraser could be:
a 25 mm
b 80 cm
c 5 m

Example

a Is table B **more than half** or **less than half** the length of table A?

Answer: Table B is **less than half** the length of table A.

b Estimate the length of table B.

Answer: Table B is about 60 cm.

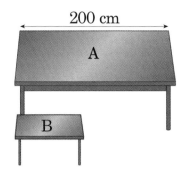

Exercise 5:3

For each question write down:

a if the length of B is **more than half** or **less than half** the length of A

b your estimate for the length of B.

1

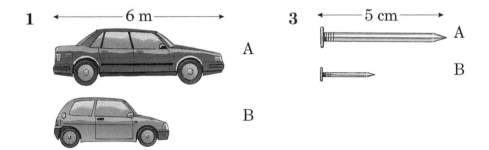

3 ← 5 cm → A

B

2

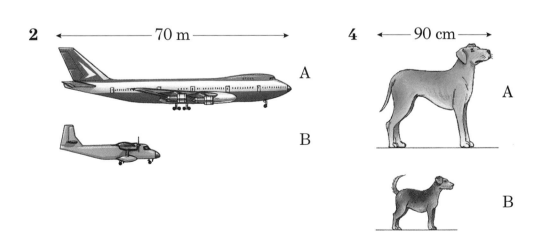

4 ← 90 cm → A

B

Example   Estimate the height of the tree.

a Mark the height of the bush on a piece of paper.

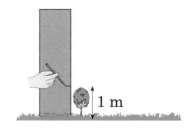

1 m

b Mark how many times this height will fit the height of the tree.

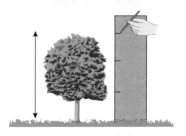

The height of the tree is 3 times the height of the bush.

Estimated height of tree $= 3 \times 1\,\text{m} = 3\,\text{m}$

Exercise 5:4

H 2

In each picture, estimate the missing length. You can use paper to help you.

1 a

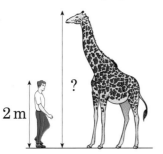

2 m   ?

b

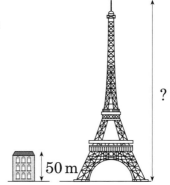

50 m   ?

2 a

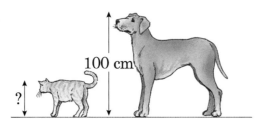

100 cm   ?

b

20 m   ?

2 New for old

The car and the bikes together have a height of 2 m.

Only things under 6 feet can get into the car park.

Can this car get in?

Length

There are two systems of measuring length.

Older system: **Imperial**
inch
foot
yard
mile

New system: **Metric**
millimetres (**mm**)
centimetres (**cm**)
metres (**m**)
kilometres (**km**)

Exercise 5:5

1 An inch is about the measurement of the top part of the thumb.

Is the top part of your thumb longer or shorter than 1 inch?

2 Which of your fingers measures nearest to 1 cm across, **a**, **b**, **c**, **d** or **e**?

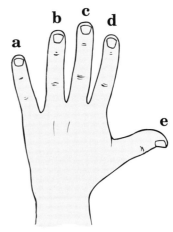

Example   Measure this line in   **a** mm   **b** cm   **c** inches.

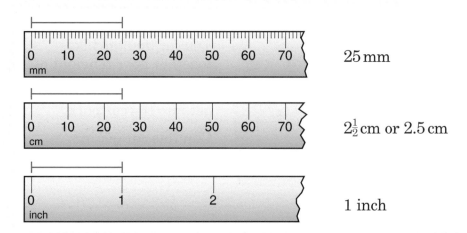

25 mm

$2\frac{1}{2}$ cm or 2.5 cm

1 inch

H 3

3   You will need rulers that measure in mm, cm and inches.
Measure these lines.
Write your answers in mm, cm, inches.

a ⊢————————————⊣ … mm … cm … inches.

b ⊢——————————————————————⊣
… mm … cm … inches.

c ⊢————————————————————⊣
… mm … cm … inches.

You should have found that: **1 cm = 10 mm**

Example

a Change 3 cm to mm.   **b** Change 40 mm to cm.

4   Which is the smallest: 1 inch, 1 cm or 1 mm?

5   How many mm are there in
   a 1 cm   **b** 2 cm   **c** 5 cm   **d** 10 cm   **e** 15 cm?

6   How many cm is the same length as
   a 20 mm   **b** 60 mm   **c** 90 mm   **d** 120 mm?

- Estimate the lengths of the following objects in centimetres. Write down your estimates on the worksheet.

Length of your pencil

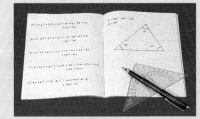

Length of your exercise book

Height of a mug

Height of your chair

- Check your estimates by measuring the objects in centimetres. Write down the actual measurements on your worksheet. Fill in the difference column.

- Choose 4 objects of your own. Estimate each length and then check by measuring. Write your answers on the worksheet.

Exercise 5:6

1   Three possible answers are given for the questions below. Write down the most sensible one.

a The length of a garden fork.

b The width of a TV set.

c The length of a knife.

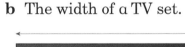

a   10 cm   100 cm   1000 cm

b   5 cm   50 cm   500 cm

c   200 cm   2 cm   20 cm

A **foot** measures 12 inches
or about   30 centimetres

2

Can you find anyone whose foot measures 12 inches, or about
30 cm, wearing shoes?
What is the length of the shortest foot you measured?
What is the length of the longest foot you measured?

Imperial
A door measures just over 6 feet.

Metric
A door measures about 2 metres.

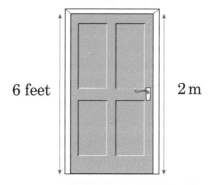

6 feet   2 m

1 metre is just over 3 feet.   feet ⟶ ÷3 ⟶ metres

Example

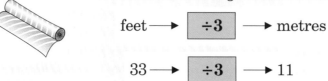

This roll contains 33 feet of wallpaper.
About how many metres is this?

feet ⟶ ÷3 ⟶ metres

33 ⟶ ÷3 ⟶ 11

The roll contains about 11 metres of wallpaper.

Exercise 5:7

Estimate these lengths in metres.
Divide the number of feet by 3.

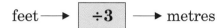

feet ⟶ ÷3 ⟶ metres

1 a

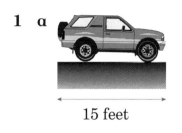

15 feet

15 feet → ÷3 → ... metres

b

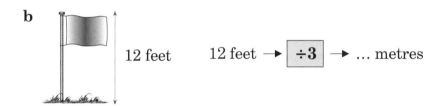

12 feet

12 feet → ÷3 → ... metres

c

30 ft
hosepipe
£25

30 feet → ÷3 → ... metres

d

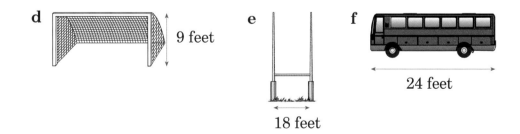

9 feet

e

18 feet

f

24 feet

2 Three possible answers are given for the questions below.
Write down the most sensible one.
Remember, the height of a door is about 2 metres, just over
6 feet.

a

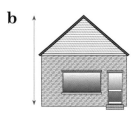

The height of a room.
3 m   10 m   20 m

b

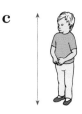

The height of a bungalow.
10 feet   20 feet   100 feet

c

The height of a 4 year old.
2 m   1 m   8 m

3 For each of the statements say whether the measurements are
sensible.
If not give a reasonable estimate.

a My teacher is 10 m tall.

b The height of my table is 5 cm.

c The width of a page of this book is 20 cm.

Metres and centimetres

1 metre = 100 cm   metres ⟶ ×100 ⟶ centimetres

Example   How many centimetres are there in 4 metres?

4 ⟶ ×100 ⟶ 400
metres   centimetres

There are 400 centimetres in 4 metres.

5   **4** Match the metres with the centimetres.
Draw a line between the matching pairs using a ruler.
One has been done for you each time.

Metres	Centimetres
5	250
1	1400
8	500
2.5	100
14	800

Centimetres	Metres
350	7
7000	25
700	9.5
950	70
2500	3.5

Another Imperial length you may come across is a yard.

   1 yard is just under 1 metre.

When measuring a football pitch in yards and metres there would be **more** yards than metres.

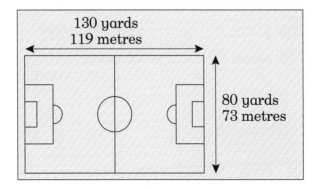

130 yards
119 metres

80 yards
73 metres

Exercise 5:8

W 6   **1** Copy the measurements and add the correct units, yards or metres.

a Rugby

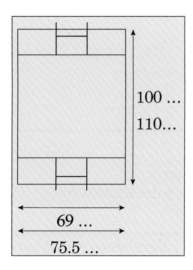

b Hockey

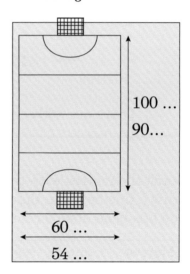

c Cricket

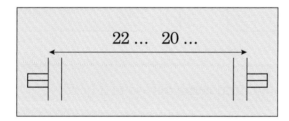

2 **a** Is 45 yards about 51 metres or 41 metres?

   b Is 200 yards about 180 metres or 210 metres?

   c Is 50 metres about 46 yards or 56 yards?

Miles and kilometres

1000 metres = 1 kilometre

A mile is **longer** than a kilometre.
There will be **more kilometres** than miles in a given distance.

5 miles is about the same distance as 8 kilometres.

In England distances are measured in miles.

In other European countries distances are measured in kilometres.

To change miles into kilometres, multiply by 1.6.

miles $\longrightarrow$ ×1.6 $\longrightarrow$ km

Example   Change 20 miles into kilometres.

20 $\longrightarrow$ ×1.6 $\longrightarrow$ 32
miles   km

32 kilometres is the same distance as 20 miles.

Exercise 5:9

You will need a calculator.

1 **a** The distance from Birmingham to London is 100 miles.
Will this distance in kilometres be **higher** or **lower** than 100?

   b Calculate the number of kilometres from Birmingham to London.

100 $\longrightarrow$ ×1.6 $\longrightarrow$ ...
miles   kilometres

2 Change these distances into kilometres.

  a Leeds to Sheffield   36 miles.

  b Manchester to London   200 miles.

  c Edinburgh to Aberdeen   125 miles.

  d Lands End to Bristol   180 miles.

3 How far is it in **a** miles **b** kilometres from your nearest big town to London?

To change kilometres into miles, divide by 1.6.

kilometres ⟶ | **÷1.6** | ⟶ miles

Example   Change 48 km into miles.

48 ⟶ | **÷1.6** | ⟶ 30
km   miles

30 miles is the same distance as 48 km.

4 Change these French distances into miles.

  a Calais to Paris   296 km.
  b Nice to Bordeaux   808 km.
  c Lyon to Dunkirk   176 km.
  d Le Havre to Cherbourg   232 km.
  e Paris to Toulouse   696 km.

5 Write the correct unit, miles or kilometres, next to the distances.
  a Bristol to Exeter   135 ...... or   216 ......
  b Leeds to Nottingham   192 ...... or   120 ......
  c Birmingham to Manchester   120 ...... or   75 ......

G 1, 2

Weight

There are two systems of measuring weight.

Older system: **Imperial**
ounce
pound
stone

New system: **Metric**
gram (**g**)
kilogram (**kg**)
1000 g = 1 kg

1 ounce is about 30 g.
1 pound is just under 500 g.

A bag of sugar weighs just over 2 lb.

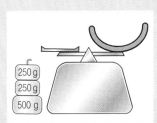

You will need some
weighing scales.

Your teacher will select 5 or more objects.

W 7

- Place the objects in what you think is the order of their weight starting with the lightest.

- Estimate the weight of each object in either grams or kilograms. Write down your estimates on the worksheet.

- Check your estimates by weighing each object. Write down the actual weights on your worksheet.

W 8

- Find objects that weigh approximately the amounts below. Write your answers on the worksheet.

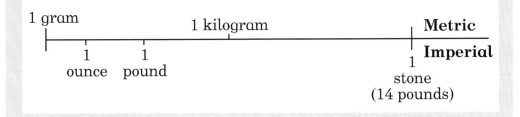

Exercise 5:10

1 Three possible answers are given for the questions below.
Write down the most sensible one.

a The weight of a packet of biscuits.

b The weight of a newborn baby.

c The weight of a microwave oven.

1 kg   225 g   10 g   100 kg   3 kg   15 kg   80 g   8 kg   80 kg

2 For each of these statements say whether the measurements are sensible.
If not give a reasonable estimate.

a Three 10 p pieces weigh 500 g.

b I can lift 4 kg.

c A bag of sugar weighs 5 grams.

d A large sack of compost weighs 20 kg.

3 Perimeter

This is a 1500 m race.

The track is only 400 m.

How many laps do they run?

Perimeter   The total distance around the outside edges of a shape is called its **perimeter**.

Example   Find the perimeter of this shape:

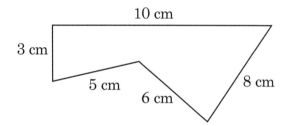

Add up the lengths:

$10\,cm + 8\,cm + 6\,cm + 5\,cm + 3\,cm = 32\,cm$

The perimeter is 32 cm.

Exercise 5:11

Find the perimeter of each of these shapes:

1

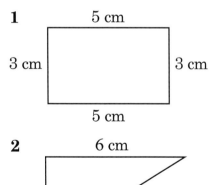

2

3

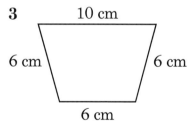

4

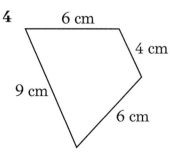

When finding a perimeter we sometimes first need to find the lengths of sides not marked.

Examples

1

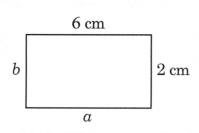

For the perimeter we need to know the lengths of a and b.

$a = 6$ cm, $b = 2$ cm, as the shape is a rectangle.

The perimeter $= 6 + 2 + 6 + 2 = 16$ cm.

2

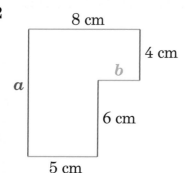

First we need to find the lengths of a and b.

$$a = 6 + 4 \qquad 8 = 5 + b$$
$$= 10 \text{ cm} \qquad b = 8 - 5$$
$$= 3 \text{ cm}$$

The perimeter $= 8 + 4 + 3 + 6 + 5 + 10$
$$= 36 \text{ cm}$$

Exercise 5:12

In each question find the lengths of a and b and then the perimeter of each shape.

1

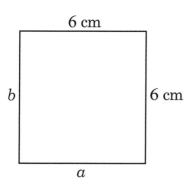

The length of a is ... cm
The length of b is ... cm
The perimeter =
$... + ... + ... + ... = ...$ cm

2

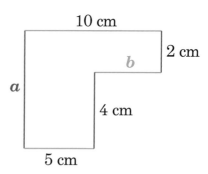

$$a = ... + ... \qquad 10 = 5 + b$$
$$= ... \text{ cm} \qquad b = ... - ...$$
$$= ... \text{ cm}$$

The perimeter =
$... + ... + ... + ... + ... + ... = ...$ cm

3

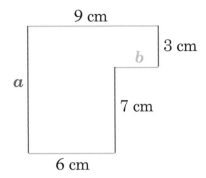

9 cm

3 cm

b

a

7 cm

6 cm

4

5 cm

3 cm

10 cm

6 cm

b

a

5   A rectangular field measures 60 m by 40 m.
A farmer wants to put a fence around its perimeter.
Draw a plan of the field.
Write the measurements on the plan.
Find the length of the fence.

6   This building site must have
a fence around it.
The fence panels are 2 m wide.

   a Work out the number of
panels needed for each
length.

   b How many panels will be
needed altogether.

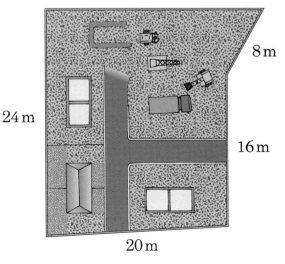

24 m

8 m

24 m

16 m

20 m

Exercise 5:13

Perimeters and tiles

You will need square tiles for this exercise.

The tile has a perimeter of 4.

You can join two tiles edge to edge like this:
This shape has a perimeter of 6.

You can join them corner to corner like this:
This shape has a perimeter of 8.

You are not allowed to join the tiles in any other way.

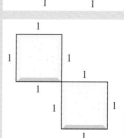

With two tiles:
6 is the smallest perimeter you can make,
8 is the biggest perimeter you can make.

1 Use three tiles.
   a Draw as many different arrangements of three tiles as you can.
   b Write down the perimeter under each one.
   c Colour the shape with the longest perimeter in red.
   d Colour the shape with the shortest perimeter in green.

2 This time using four tiles, follow the same instructions as in question **1**.

3 Using five tiles, draw only:
   a the arrangement with the longest perimeter
   b the arrangement with the shortest perimeter.

4 Put your results in a table.

Number of tiles	Longest perimeter	Shortest perimeter
2	8	6
3		
4		
5		

1 Estimate George's age for each of the times he moved house.

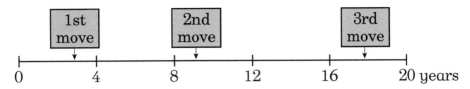

2 Estimate the winters in which Britain had heavy snowfalls.

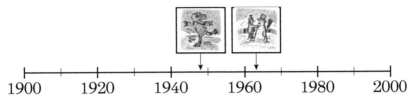

3 Write the correct units, mm, cm, m or km, for each picture.

a

Swansea to Cardiff 60 ...

c

Drawing pin 9 ...

b

Scissors 15 ...

d

Washing line 11 ...

4 In each picture below estimate the missing length.

a

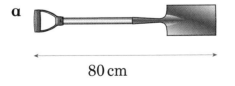

80 cm

?

b

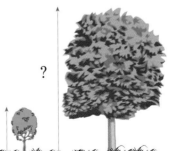

?

2 m

5 Write down the measurement of this line in **a** mm **b** cm **c** inches.

——————————

6 To change inches into centimetres:

inches ⟶ | ×2.5 | ⟶ centimetres

How many centimetres are there in **a** 4 inches **b** 10 inches?

7 Write down which is the longest from each of these pairs.
a 1 inch or 1 centimetre.
b 1 yard or 1 metre.
c 1 mile or 1 kilometre.

8 To change miles into kilometres:

miles ⟶ | ×1.6 | ⟶ kilometres

How many kilometres are there in **a** 15 miles **b** 100 miles?

9 Which is heavier 1 gram or 1 kilogram?

10 Write grams (g) or kilograms (kg), whichever is more sensible, for the following weights:

a
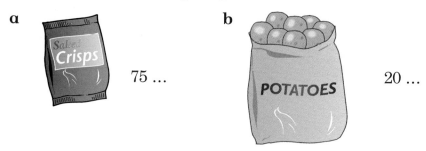
75 ...

b
20 ...

11 Find the perimeter of each of these shapes.

a

b First find side marked x.
Then find the perimeter.

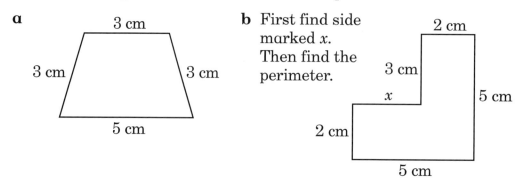

6 Volume

QUESTIONS

Many scientists believe that global warming is melting the polar ice caps.

A study by the Inter-governmental Panel for Climate Change estimates that by the year 2070 global sea level could be as much as 71 cm higher than it is now.

Find out which parts of the UK would be underwater.

1 Units of capacity

Milk comes in two different sizes.
There is a scale on the side of this carton.
It tells you how many litres the carton holds.
The scale on this carton goes up in litres.

This carton holds 4 litres.   This carton holds 1 litre.

Exercise 6:1

1 **a** Glenroy has a full 4 litre carton of milk.
How many 1 litre cartons is this equal to?

   b Sareena's carton of milk is not full.
How many litres of milk are in the carton?

The scale on this carton goes up in $\frac{1}{2}$ litres.

This carton is not full.

It contains $2\frac{1}{2}$ litres of milk.

2 How many litres do these cartons contain?

a 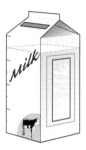   **b**    **c**

3 Some of the marks have rubbed off this carton. How many litres does the carton contain?

Yoghurt comes in two sizes.

500 ml   and   100 ml

Exercise 6:2

1 How many small yoghurt pots could you fill from one **full** large yoghurt pot?

2 The large yoghurt pots below are not full.
   How many small yoghurt pots could you fill from each one?

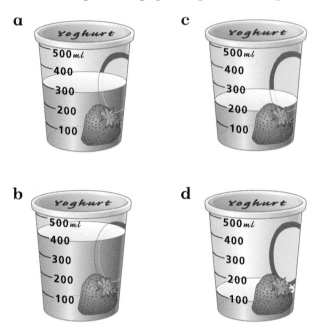

3 This fruit juice carton contains 1000 ml of juice.

   a How many 250 ml cartons will it fill?

   b Dave drinks 100 ml of juice each day.
       How many drinks will the 1000 ml carton make?

2 How many?

This pack contains three rows of four cans. This box contains 12 cans.

Exercise 6:3

1 How many cans of drink are there in each of these packs?

a

d

b

e

c

f

2 This is a four-pack of Fizzo. How many four-packs can you fill from this group of cans?

3   How many boxes of fruit juice are in each of these packs?

a

d

b

e

c

f

4   This milk bottle
    crate holds 6 bottles.

How many crates could
you fill with these bottles?

Exercise 6:4

You are going to arrange cubes to make solids.
Use your cubes to make the shape in each picture.
Write down the number of cubes that you use for each solid.

1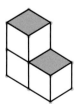

2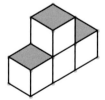

Shape **1** used ... cubes.

Shape **2** used ... cubes.

3

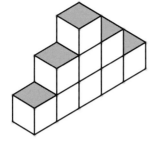

4

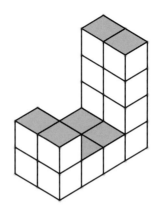

5 This solid is made
from 8 cubes.
Which two other solids are
made from 8 cubes?

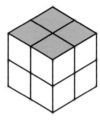

a

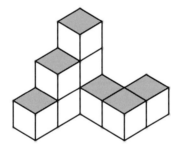

c

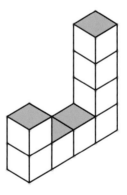

b

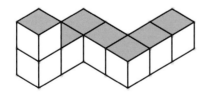

 1

6 a Make four other solids from 8 cubes.

b Draw the solids on triangular dotted paper.

3 Volume of a cuboid

A cube that has sides of 1 cm is called a 1 cm cube.
You say that it has a **volume** of **1 cm cubed**.
You write this as **1 cm³**.

This shape is made from
2 cubes.
Its **volume** is **2 cm³**.

This shape is made from
5 cubes.
Its **volume** is **5 cm³**.

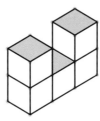

Exercise 6:5

Jenny made these shapes with 1 cm cubes.
What is the volume of each shape?

1

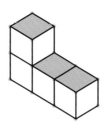

Volume = ... cm³

3

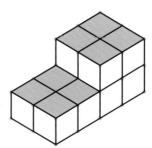

2

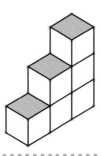

4

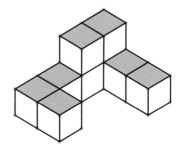

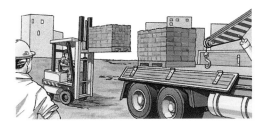

The builder needs to know how many bricks there are in each pack.

Exercise 6:6

 1 All of these solids are made with 1 cm cubes.
Make each of the solids.
Find the volume. Write your answers in cm^3.

1

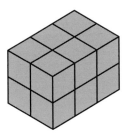

3

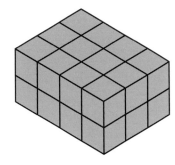

2

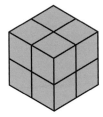

4

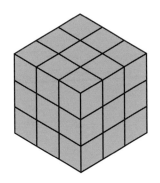

The blocks above are all **cuboids**.
Instead of counting cubes you can **calculate** the volume.

Write down the length, width and height of the sides.

$$\text{Volume} = \textit{l}\text{ength} \times \textit{w}\text{idth} \times \textit{h}\text{eight}$$
$$= \textit{l} \times \textit{w} \times \textit{h}$$
$$= 5 \times 2 \times 3$$
$$= 30 \text{ cm}^3$$

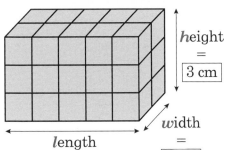

height
=
3 cm

width
=
2 cm

length
=
5 cm

---

5 (1) Make each of these solids.

(2) Write down the length, width and height of each solid.

(3) Calculate the volume using: volume = length × width × height.

(4) Check that the answer is the same by counting.

a

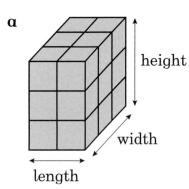

height

width

length

c

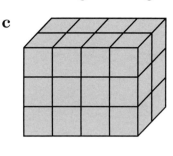

b

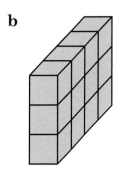

d

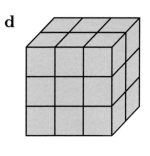

Exercise 6:7

Work out how many cans there are in each of these packs.

1

2

We do not need to count the cubes to work out the volume of a cuboid.
We can just use the fast way of calculating the volume.

Volume of a cuboid

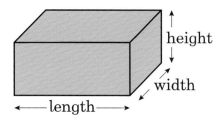

Volume of a cuboid = *l*ength × *w*idth × *h*eight

Example   Find the volume of this cuboid:

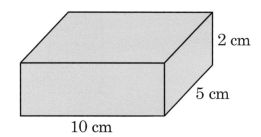

2 cm

5 cm

10 cm

Volume = *l*ength × *w*idth × *h*eight
     =   *l*   ×   *w*   ×   *h*
     =   10   ×   5   ×   2
     = 100 cm^3

Exercise 6:8

Work out the volume of these cuboids.

1

2 cm

2 cm

3 cm

2

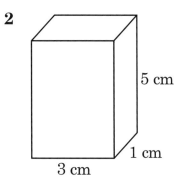

5 cm

1 cm

3 cm

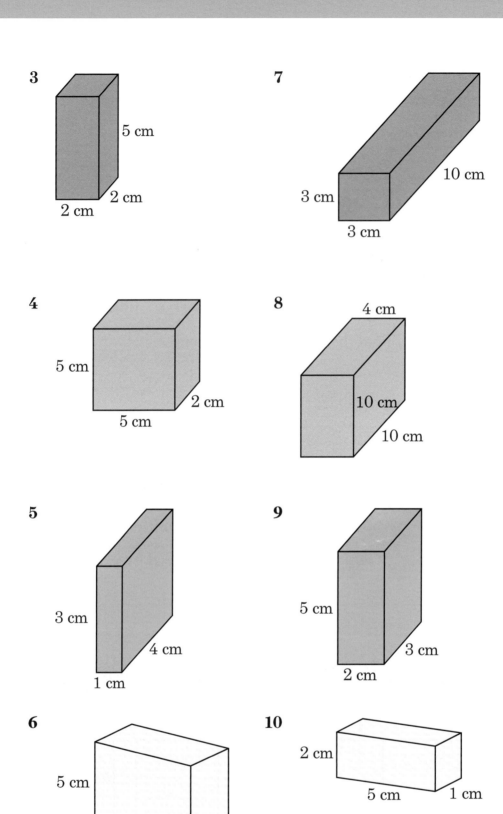

3 5 cm 2 cm 2 cm

7 10 cm 3 cm 3 cm

4 5 cm 5 cm 2 cm

8 4 cm 10 cm 10 cm

5 3 cm 4 cm 1 cm

9 5 cm 3 cm 2 cm

6 5 cm 6 cm 2 cm

10 2 cm 5 cm 1 cm

Exercise 6:9

Work out the volume of these containers.
You might need a calculator.

1

4

2

5

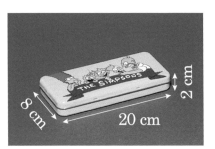

3

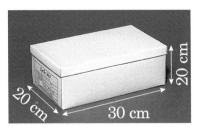

6

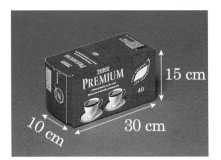

Design a box

The Happy Cow Cheese Company wants a box for 12 Happy Cheeses.

Each of the cheeses is a cube of side 2 cm.

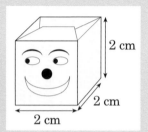

1 What is the volume of one cheese?

$$\textbf{Volume} = \textbf{\textit{l}} \times \textbf{\textit{w}} \times \textbf{\textit{h}}$$
$$= \ldots \times \ldots \times \ldots$$
$$= \ldots \text{cm}^3$$

2 This is one possible arrangement
of the 12 cheeses in a cuboid.
What is the volume of this cuboid?

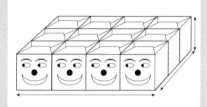

$$\textbf{Volume} = \textbf{\textit{l}} \times \textbf{\textit{w}} \times \textbf{\textit{h}}$$
$$= \ldots \times \ldots \times \ldots$$
$$= \ldots \text{cm}^3$$

3 Use 12 cubes to make a different cuboid.
Draw your cuboid.
Calculate the volume of your cuboid.

4 Make as many different cuboids as you can out of 12 cubes.
Draw each cuboid.
Calculate the volume of each cuboid.

5 Write a sentence about the volumes of the cuboids.

6 The Happy Cow Cheese Company is going to choose one
arrangement as the box for 12 cheeses.
Which one would you suggest they choose? Say why.

7 The Happy Cow Cheese Company might decide to sell boxes
with a different number of cheeses.
Design a cuboid for 6, 16 and 20 cheeses.

1 How many cups will these jugs fill?

a  **b**  **c**

d  **e**  **f**

2 A doctor gives medicine to some children.
Each child has one 5 ml spoonful.
How many 5 ml spoonfuls are there in these beakers?

a   **b** 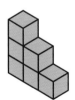 **c**

3 All of these shapes are made with 1 cm cubes.
What is the volume of each shape?

a **b** **c**

4 All of these cuboids are made with 1 cm cubes.
Find the volume of each. Write your answers in cm^3.

a   **b**   **c**

5 Calculate the volume of each of these cuboids.
Write your answers in cm³.

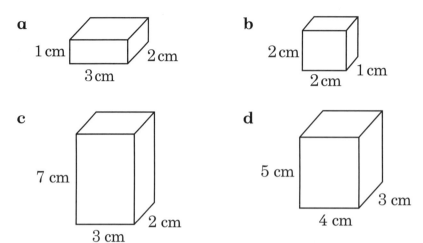

a 1 cm 2 cm 3 cm

b 2 cm 2 cm 1 cm

c 7 cm 2 cm 3 cm

d 5 cm 3 cm 4 cm

6 Calculate the volume of each of these cuboids.

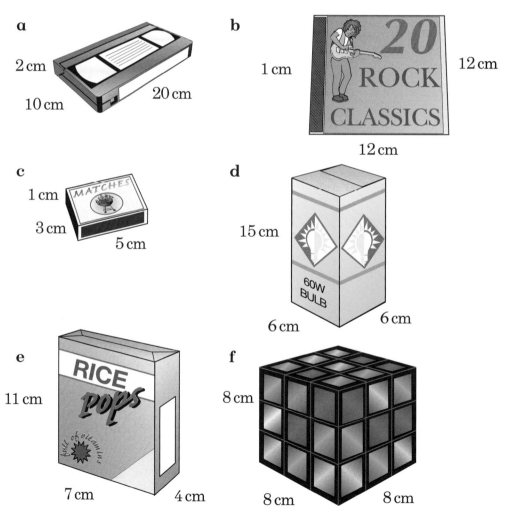

a 2 cm 10 cm 20 cm

b 1 cm 12 cm 12 cm

c 1 cm 3 cm 5 cm

d 15 cm 6 cm 6 cm

e 11 cm 7 cm 4 cm

f 8 cm 8 cm 8 cm

7 Decimals

QUESTIONS

In printed maths we don't use commas in numbers. Why is this?

1 Tenths and hundredths

Numbers are written in columns.
The column that the digit is in tells you its value.
This is known as the **place value**.

Example   The number 4368 is on a place value grid.

Thousands 1000s	Hundreds 100s	Tens 10s	Units 1s
4	3	6	8

4 is 4 thousands or 4000	3 is 3 hundreds or 300	6 is 6 tens or 60	8 is 8 units or 8

Exercise 7:1

1 What is the value of the 4 in the number 234?

2 What is the value of the 5 in the number 521?

3 What is the value of the figure 7 in 1476?

4 What is the value of the figure 9 in the number 3958?

5 What is the value of the figure 2 in the number 2698?

6 What is the value of the 8 in 128?

Numbers before a decimal point are whole numbers.
Numbers after a decimal point are parts of a unit.

Tenths   One unit can be split into 10 equal parts.
These are called **tenths** and can be written as a decimal.

0.1	0.1	0.1	0.1	0.1	0.1	0.1	0.1	0.1	0.1

Example   The shape below represents one unit divided into tenths.
Write as a decimal how much is shaded.

6 of the parts are green.
This is 0.6 of one unit.

Exercise 7:2

1 Each shape below is split into 10 equal parts.
For each shape, write as a decimal how much is shaded green.

a **c**

b **d**

We can also use circles to represent 1 unit.

One whole circle is shaded and
0.3 of the other circle is shaded.

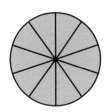 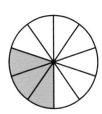

We can write this as: **1** **.** **3**

---

2 In each question write down the total amount that is shaded green.

a **c**

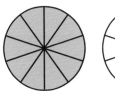

... **.** ... ... **.** ...

b **d**

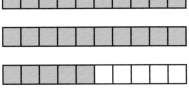 

... **.** ...

... **.** ...

This ruler is used to measure in centimetres.
Tenths are marked on the ruler.

Each small section represents 0.1
Ten small sections make up one centimetre.

The value marked X is 0.9 cm
The value marked Y is 2.7 cm

3 Write down the values marked by the arrows.

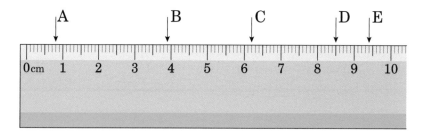

W 1   **4** Mark the following values on the ruler.

    P = 2.3 cm   Q = 3.7 cm   R = 4.8 cm   S = 5.1 cm

5 Measure the lines as accurately as you can. Write your answers
in centimetres.
The first one has been done for you.

  a ├────────────┤   *4.3 cm*

  b ├──────────────────────┤

  c ├─────────────────────────┤

  d ├──────┤

W 1   **6** Place these decimals on the number line.
0.8 has been done for you.

    0.8, 0.1, 0.5, 1.3, 1.6, 1.9

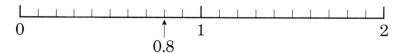

Tenths can be added to the place value grid.

Example   **a** Thirty seven and two tenths can be written as 37.2
This is called a decimal.

Tens 10s	Units 1s	•	Tenths 0.1s
3	7	•	2

b Write eight tenths as a decimal.

Eight tenths written as a decimal is 0.8

Exercise 7:3

1 Write the following numbers as decimals.

a Four and three tenths.

b Twenty-seven and eight tenths.

c Nine tenths.

d One hundred and three tenths.

e Two and nine tenths.

f Fifty-eight and seven tenths.

2 What is the value of the 7 in 5.7?

3 What is the value of the 9 in 8.9?

We often call the tenths column the first decimal place.
2.9 is a number with 1 decimal place.

Hundredths   **Hundredths** come from splitting 1 unit into 100 equal parts.

Each square on this page is split into 100 equal parts.

Each part is called a **hundredth**. As a decimal this is **0.01**

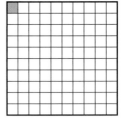

Example

How much of the square is coloured green?

27 parts are coloured green.

This is 27 hundredths or 2 tenths and 7 hundredths.

Written as a decimal this is 0.27 of a whole.

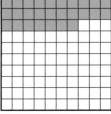

27 hundredths

The place value grid can be extended to include hundredths.

Tens 10s	Units 1s	Tenths 0.1s	Hundredths 0.01s
	0	2	7

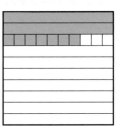

2 tenths and 7 hundredths

Exercise 7:4

1 How much of each shape is shaded green? Write your answers as decimals.

a 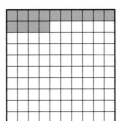   b 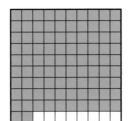   c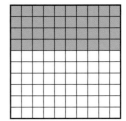

 2

2 Colour in the parts to show these decimals.
  a 0.32   **c** 0.5   **e** 0.14
  b 0.84   **d** 0.7   **f** 0.94

	Units 1s	Tenths 0.1s	Hundredths 0.01s
Example Write as a decimal			
a two tenths and five hundredths **a**	0	2	5
b twenty-eight hundredths. **b**	0	2	8

3 Write the following as decimals.
   a Four tenths and five hundredths. **d** Thirty-six hundredths.
   b Eight tenths and nine hundredths. **e** Seven hundredths.
   c Nine tenths and one hundredth. **f** Three hundredths.

Example Place these decimals on a line from 4.9 to 5.1

4.93, 4.99, 5.01, 5.06

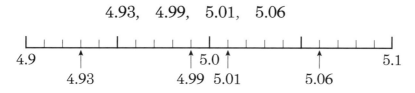

Example Write down a decimal between 5.3 and 5.4

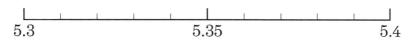

You may choose **any** decimal that lies between 5.3 and 5.4 as shown on the number line

For example 5.34, 5.38 etc.

Exercise 7:5

 1 Place these decimals on the number lines provided.
   a 2.32 2.48 2.45 2.5   **c** 4.95 5.08 4.91 5.01
   b 6.78 6.83 6.71 6.89   **d** 10.91 11.05 10.99 11.09

2 Write down a decimal between:
   a 3.8 and 3.9   **c** 1.2 and 1.3
   b 2.4 and 2.5   **d** 6.7 and 6.8

2 Getting things in order

Examples

a Which is smaller 3.12 or 4.34?

First look at the **whole number before** the decimal point.

Whole numbers	Decimal point	Tenths	Hundredths
3	•	1	2
4	•	3	4

3 is smaller than **4**

3.12 is smaller than **4**.34

Where the whole numbers are the same we need to look at the figures after the decimal point **in order**.

Examples

a Which is smaller   13.42 or 13.63?

The figures are the same until the **first** figure after the decimal points.

13.**4**2 is smaller than 13.**6**3

b Which is smaller   3.457 or 3.429?

The figures are the same until the **second** figure after the decimal point.

13.4**2**9 is smaller than 3.4**5**7

Exercise 7:6

1 Which is smaller?
  a 5.2 or 6.7   **d** 3.46 or 3.48   **g** 23.563 or 23.565
  b 14.8 or 13.9   **e** 8.43 or 8.12   **h** 11.245 or 11.249
  c 7.3 or 7.1   **f** 6.9 or 6.71   **i** 23.78 or 23.772

2 Put these numbers in order of size starting with the smallest
  a 24.1   24.4   23.9   **c** 6.875   6.889   6.879
  b 13.12   13.15   13.11   **d** 15.243   15.372   15.283

Less than and greater than

< means **less than**   > means **greater than**

Example   Place either < or > in the statement to make it correct.

4 ☐ 6   Answer: 4 │<│ 6

Exercise 7:7

 1 Place either < or > in the statement to make it correct.

a 7 ☐ 3   **d** 5 + 4 ☐ 5 × 2

b 6 ☐ 10   **e** 16 − 5 ☐ 4 × 6

c 9 ☐ 2   **f** 3 + 6 + 7 ☐ 20 − 7

Example   Place either < or > in the statement to make it correct.

a 3.9 ☐ 3.6   Answer: 3.9 │>│ 3.6

b 3.92 ☐ 3.96   Answer: 3.92 │<│ 3.96

---

 2 Place either < or > in the statement to make it correct.

a 4.2 ☐ 3.8   **d** 6.57 ☐ 6.54

b 5.6 ☐ 5.5   **e** 4.8 ☐ 4.9

c 8.32 ☐ 8.36   **f** 9.82 ☐ 9.79

3 These are the distances in metres jumped by six Year 9 girls in the long jump final.

Rajual	3.25	Rona	3.76
Alison	3.48	Jo	4.12
Sophie	2.90	Fiona	3.95

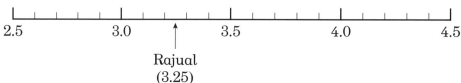

Rajual
(3.25)

a Copy the number line and write the names in the correct place. (Names can go either side of the line).

The longest jump wins the competition.

b What distance did the winner jump?

c Who came second?

d Who came third? What distance did she jump?

4 These are the distances in metres jumped by six Year 9 boys in the long jump final.

Wayne	4.28	Churchill	4.62
Royston	3.48	Alan	4.09
Tim	2.90	Dave	3.95

```
2.5      3.0      3.5      4.0   ↑  4.5      5.0
                                Wayne
                                (4.28)
```

a Copy the number line.
Use the number line to show how far each boy jumped.

The longest jump wins the competition.

b What distance did the winner jump?

c Who came second?

d Who came third? What distance did he jump?

3 Working with decimals

Adding decimals without a calculator

It is useful to know the number of tenths
needed to make the next whole number.

Example

0.8 + 0.2

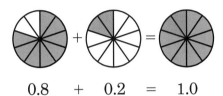

0.8 + 0.2 = 1.0

Exercise 7:8

4 **1** Work these out.

    a 0.6 + 0.4

    b 1.5 + 0.5

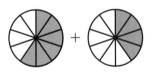

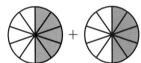

    c 1.8 + 0.2   **d** 3.3 + 0.7   **e** 4.9 + 0.1

5 **2** Find the missing number.

    a $0.7 + \boxed{} = 1.0$ **c** $5.1 + \boxed{} = 6.0$

    b $2.3 + \boxed{} = 3.0$ **d** $3.8 + \boxed{} = 4.0$

Example

$1.7 + \boxed{?} = 2.0$

A number line can be used.

0.3

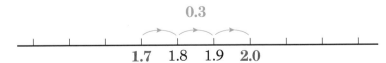

1.7 1.8 1.9 2.0

Answer: $\boxed{?} = 0.3$

Example

Sam travels to school by bus.
He walks 0.8 miles to catch the bus.
When he gets off the bus he walks 0.5 miles to school.

How far does he walk altogether?

0.8 miles + 0.5 miles

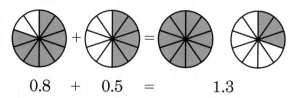

0.8   +   0.5   =   1.3

A number line can be used.

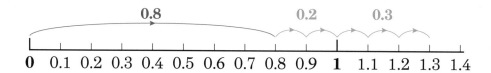

0.8 miles + 0.5 miles = 1.3 miles. Sam walks 1.3 miles altogether.

Exercise 7:9

1 Find the total distances. The numbers are given in miles.
Use a number line to help you.

  a 0.3 + 0.5   **c** 0.6 + 0.8   **e** 0.9 + 0.6   **g** 0.7 + 0.5
  b 0.4 + 0.3   **d** 0.9 + 0.2   **f** 0.8 + 0.7   **h** 0.4 + 0.9

2 You can also add decimals using columns as you do with whole
numbers. The decimal points must be in line.
The first question is done for you.

  a   0.9   **c**   2.4   **e**   0.6   **g**   1.8
        + 0.2   + 1.8   + 3.4   + 2.7
        ─────   ─────   ─────   ─────
          1.1

  b   0.4   **d**   1.9   **f**   4.3   **h**   4.5
        + 0.9   + 2.2   + 1.9   + 3.8
        ─────   ─────   ─────   ─────

136

Subtracting decimals

Paul catches the bus at the same stop as Sam.
The bus stop is 0.8 miles from Sam's house and 1 mile from Paul's.

How much further does Paul walk to the stop?

Work out $1.0 - 0.8$ (a mile can be written as 1.0 mile).

Use a number line

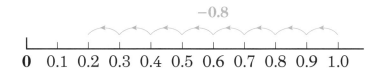

$1.0 - 0.8 = 0.2$ miles.

Exercise 7:10

1 Subtract these distances given in miles.
You may use a number line to help you.

    a $1.0 - 0.3$ **d** $1.0 - 0.8$

    b $1.0 - 0.6$ **e** $1.0 - 0.9$

    c $1.0 - 0.5$ **f** $1.0 - 0.7$

2 You can also subtract decimals using columns as you do with
whole numbers. The decimal points must be in line.
The first question is done for you.

	a	2.6	**c**	4.6	**e**	7.6	**g**	3.1
		$-\ 1.4$		$-\ 3.2$		$-\ 1.1$		$-\ 1.9$
		$\overline{1.2}$						

	b	4.9	**d**	5.7	**f**	6.8	**h**	7.2
		$-\ 3.3$		$-\ 2.4$		$-\ 4.3$		$-\ 2.6$

4 Estimating

100 000 attend Festival

Traffic was in chaos yesterday as 100 000 people arrived at Festival Park for an open air concert. Organisers were amazed at the number of people who came.

The attendance is given as 100 000.
This does not mean that exactly 100 000 people came.
The number has been rounded to give a sensible estimate.
It would be silly for the paper to say 106 896 people came to the concert!

Rounding

Example   Round 6.7 to the nearest whole number.

6.7 is nearer to 7 than to 6.
6.7 is rounded to 7.

Exercise 7:11

1   Round these numbers to the nearest whole number.
    .5 is always rounded **up** to the next number.

a 5.7	**d** 9.4	**g** 13.7	**j** 34.7
b 3.6	**e** 4.5	**h** 23.6	**k** 46.5
c 7.1	**f** 9.8	**i** 24.2	**l** 58.5

Example   Round 74 to the nearest 10.

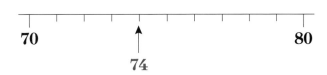

74 is nearer to 70 than to 80.
74 is rounded to 70.

---

2 Round these numbers to the nearest 10.
Remember 5 is always rounded **up**.

a 16	**d** 54	**g** 98	**j** 63
b 34	**e** 67	**h** 14	**k** 36
c 87	**f** 35	**i** 56	**l** 55

Example   Round 650 to the nearest 100.

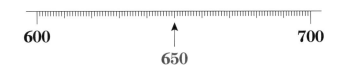

650 is halfway between 600 and 700.
650 is rounded **up** to 700.

---

3 Round these numbers to the nearest 100.

a 267	**d** 452	**g** 989	**j** 603
b 356	**e** 849	**h** 350	**k** 239
c 543	**f** 719	**i** 427	**l** 450

Sometimes when multiplying there are ways of making the calculations easier so you can work out the sum in your head.

Example

The cost of an Allday breakfast is £2.99
How much would it cost for 5 Allday breakfasts?

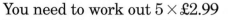

You need to work out $5 \times £2.99$
It is easier to find $5 \times £3$ and then take off $5 \times 1\,\text{p}$.

$$5 \times £3 = £15$$
$$5 \times 1\,\text{p} = 5\,\text{p}$$
so $\quad 5 \times £2.99 = £15 - 5\,\text{p}$
$$= £14.95$$

Exercise 7:12

Calculate the following using the method shown in the example.

1 $5 \times £9.99$

$5 \times £...... = £......$
$5 \times ...\,\text{p} \quad = ...\,\text{p}$
$5 \times £9.99 = ... - ......$
$\qquad\qquad = ...$

2 $3 \times £4.98$

$3 \times £... \quad = £...$
$3 \times ...\,\text{p} \quad = ...\,\text{p}$
$3 \times £4.98 = ... - ...$
$\qquad\qquad = ...$

3 $6 \times £2.99$ **4** $5 \times £99$

Try to work these out in your head

5 $4 \times £5.05$ **6** $3 \times £7.05$

You often use your calculator to do questions.
First estimate your answer.
It is very easy to hit the wrong key.

Example   Work out 5.4×179

To check that your answer is sensible, round your numbers.

Estimate: 5.4   ×   179
             ↓   ↓
          nearest   nearest
           whole   hundred
          number
             ↓   ↓
            5   ×   200 = 1000

Now work out the exact answer.

5 **.** **4** **×** **1** **7** **9** **=**   Answer: 966.6

The estimate of 1000 is near to 966.6, so the answer is probably right.

Exercise 7:13

You will need a calculator.

W 5,6

Estimate your answers by rounding your numbers.
Calculate the exact answer on your calculator.
Does your exact answer look sensible?

1 a   6.1   ×   19   **b**   11   ×   9.8

        6.1   ×   19   11   ×   9.8
         ↓   ↓   ↓   ↓
      nearest   nearest   nearest   nearest
       whole   ten   ten   whole
      number   number
         ↓   ↓   ↓   ↓
        ...   ×   ... = ...   ×   ... = ...

Exact answer: $6.1 \times 19 = ...$ Exact answer: $11 \times 9.8 = ...$

2 Work these out in the same way.
   a 6.3×9.7 **c** 4.9×3.2 **e** 47×33
   b 67×23 **d** 36×2.4 **f** 71×129

1 What is the value of the figure 6 in these numbers

   a 216   **b** 612   **c** 3.6

W7   2 Colour in the parts to show these decimals on the worksheet.

   a 0.15   **b** 0.7   **c** 0.83

3 Write the following numbers as decimals.

   a Three tenths and six hundredths.

   b Nine tenths and two hundredths.

W8   4 Place these numbers on the number lines.

   a 2.6,   2.3,   2.1,   2.5

   b 3.42,   3.48,   3.54,   3.36

5 Which is smaller?

   a 4.6 or 3.2   **d** 4.789 or 4.783

   b 7.8 or 7.9   **e** 2.764 or 2.78

   c 5.42 or 5.46   **f** 8.54 or 8.64

6 Place either $<$ or $>$ in the statement to make it correct.

   a 3 ☐ 5   **c** 7.62 ☐ 7.45

   b 3.8 ☐ 3.4   **d** 8.37 ☐ 8.39

7 Work these out.
You can use a number line to help you.

   a 0.4 + 0.6   **c** 2.7 + 0.3

   b 0.8 + 0.2   **d** 4.1 + 0.9

8

8 Find the missing number.
You may use a number line to help you.

a $0.3 + \boxed{} = 1.0$ **c** $4.6 + \boxed{} = 5.0$

b $0.2 + \boxed{} = 1.0$ **d** $2.7 + \boxed{} = 3.0$

9 Add these decimals.

a	3.7	**b**	5.4	**c**	6.3	**d**	1.5
	+ 1.4		+ 2.8		+ 2.8		+ 2.9

 9

10 Subtract these distances given in miles.
You may use a number line to help you.

a $1.0 - 0.4$ **c** $1.0 - 0.2$

b $1.0 - 0.7$ **d** $1.0 - 0.6$

11 Subtract these decimals

a	5.8	**b**	3.9	**c**	8.7	**d**	6.8
	− 2.6		− 1.4		− 2.5		− 1.3

12 Round these numbers to the nearest whole number.

a 5.6   **b** 3.2   **c** 18.5   **d** 23.9

13 Round these numbers to the nearest 10.

a 23   **b** 38   **c** 45   **d** 32

14 Round these numbers to the nearest 100.

a 170   **b** 243   **c** 350   **d** 517

15 Calculate £5.99 × 3.
Do not use a calculator.

W 9   **16**   Estimate your answers by rounding up your numbers.
Calculate the exact answers on your calculator.

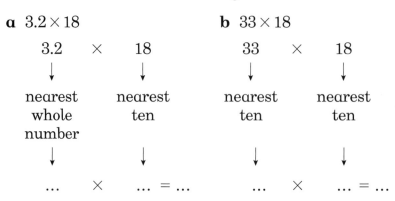

a 3.2×18

3.2	$\times$	18
↓		↓
nearest whole number		nearest ten
↓		↓
...	$\times$	... $=$ ...

Exact answer: $3.2 \times 18 =$ ...

b 33×18

33	$\times$	18
↓		↓
nearest ten		nearest ten
↓		↓
...	$\times$	... $=$ ...

Exact answer: $33 \times 18 =$ ...

8 Algebra

QUESTIONS

1	1	1	1
1	3	5	7
1	5	13	25
1	7	25	?

What is the missing number?

CORE

1 Arranging in rows

Stan the gardener wants to plant some cabbages in rows. He can arrange 6 cabbages in the following rectangles.

1 row

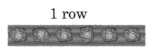

2 rows

3 rows

6 rows

We can list these arrangements in a table.

For 6 plants:	Number of rows	Number of plants in each row
	1	6
	2	3
	3	2
	6	1

The table shows the numbers that multiply together to give 6.

They could be written as:

Exercise 8:1

You can use counters to represent the plants.

 1 **a** Arrange 8 plants in:
  i one row
  ii two rows
  iii four rows
  iv eight rows.

b Draw your arrangements.

c List the arrangements in a table.

Number of rows	Number of plants in each row
1	
2	
4	
8	

d Write down the numbers that multiply together to give 8.

... ...

We need only write each pair of numbers once.

 2 Arrange 10 plants in as many different **rows** as possible.
  a Draw your arrangements.
  b Complete the table.
  c Write down the numbers that multiply together to give 10.

 3 Arrange 12 plants in as many different **rectangles** as possible.
  a Draw your arrangements.
  b Complete the table.
  c Write down the numbers that multiply together to give 12.

Factor   A number that divides exactly into another number with no remainder is called a **factor**.

Factors can be found by arranging counters into rectangles.

from the table for 6 plants:

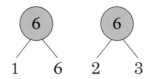

We need only write each pair of numbers once.

The factors of 6 are   1,   2,   3,   6

This can be written as:

factors of 6 = {1,   2,   3,   6}

Exercise 8:2

H 1   For questions **1** to **3** use your answers on Worksheet 1.

1   **a** Write down all the **factors** of 8.
    b Copy and complete:

factors of 8 = {1,   ...,   ...,   8}

2   **a** Write down all the **factors** of 10.
    b Copy and complete:

factors of 10 = {...,   ...,   ...,   ...}

3   **a** Write down all the **factors** of 12.
    b Copy and complete:

factors of 12 = {...,   ...,   ...,   ...,   ...,   ...}

For questions **4** and **5** you may want to arrange counters in rectangles to help you answer the questions.

 4 a Write down the numbers that multiply together to give 20.

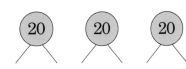

   b Write down all the factors of 20.

   c Copy and complete:

       factors of 20 = {...,   ...,   ...,   ...,   ...,   ...}

 5 a Write down the numbers that multiply together to give 18.

   b Write down all the factors of 18.

   c Copy and complete:

       factors of 18 = {...,   ...,   ...,   ...,   ...,   ...}

Prime numbers

Exercise 8:3

1 a Arrange 5 counters in as many rectangles as possible.
   b Draw any arrangements you find.
   c Write down the factors of 5.

2 a Arrange 7 counters in as many rectangles as possible.
   b Draw any arrangements you find.
   c Write down the factors of 7.

Numbers 5 and 7 each have only two factors.

Numbers that have **only two** factors are called **prime numbers**.

Prime numbers have only two factors, themselves and 1.

Example   The number 11 is a prime number because

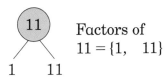

Factors of
$11 = \{1, \quad 11\}$

Remember 1 is a not a prime number because it has only one factor, 1.

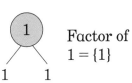

Factor of
$1 = \{1\}$

W 2 *Finding other prime numbers*

Ashley knows a way of finding all the
prime numbers less than 25.
Follow his method.

You will need the four number squares
on the worksheet.

1. **On the first number square:**
   Put a circle round the 2 and then shade all the numbers that
   are in the 2 times table.

2. **On the second number square:**
   Put a circle round the 3 and then shade all the numbers that
   are in the 3 times table.

3. **On the third number square:**
   Put a circle round the 5 and then shade all the numbers that
   are in the 5 times table.

4. **On the fourth number square:**

1	2	3	4	5
6	7	8	9	10
11	12	13	14	15
16	17	18	19	20
21	22	23	24	25

- Cross out the 1. It is not a prime number.
- Circle the number 2 and cross out all the numbers you
  crossed out on the first grid.
- Circle the number 3 and cross out all the numbers you
  crossed out on the second grid.
- Circle the number 5 and cross out all the numbers you
  crossed out on the third grid.
- Now circle all the numbers not crossed out.

List all the numbers circled – **these are the prime numbers
less than 25.**

Investigation

1 2 is the only even prime number.

What happens if you add the prime number 2 to any other prime number?

Calculate the answer when you add 2 to these prime numbers.

a $2 + 5$ **b** $2 + 7$ **c** $2 + 13$

e Are your answers odd or even?

2 By adding prime numbers you can get all the even numbers larger than 2.

Example

$2 + 2 = 4$ (you can use the same number twice) $3 + 5 = 8$

For some numbers there are several ways of doing it.

$14 = 7 + 7$ $14 = 3 + 11$ $14 = 2 + 5 + 7$

Using the prime numbers   2, 3, 5, 7, 11, 13, 17, 19, 23, write each even number from 4 to 40 as the sum of prime numbers. If you find several ways of making a number write them all down.

Set out your answers in a table similar to the one below.

Even numbers	Addition of primes
4	$2 + 2$
6	
8	$3 + 5$
10	
12	
14	$7 + 7$, $3 + 11$, $2 + 5 + 7$
16	
18	
20	

2 Dividing it up

At the end of a lesson the chairs must be stacked in piles of 3. There are 21 chairs to be stacked. Will the chairs fit into an exact number of stacks of 3?

Exercise 8:4

You will need a calculator for this exercise.

1 **a** Write down 3.

  b On your calculator press **3 + + =**

  c Write down the answer.

  d Now press **=** again.

  e Write down the answer you get.

  f Use your calculator to find the next six numbers in this pattern.

  g Write down each answer you get.

| **Multiples** | All the numbers you wrote down in question **1** are **multiples** of 3. |

This means that 3 will divide into them exactly with no remainders.

Example   3 6 9 12 15 18 21   are multiples of 3

Multiples are the same as or **bigger than** the starting number.

Because 21 is a multiple of 3 the 21 chairs will fit into an exact number of stacks of 3.

Example

Will 35 chairs fit into an exact number of
stacks of 5?

a Write down 5.

b On your calculator press   **5** **+** **+** **=**

c Write down the answer.

d Now press **=** again.

e Write down the answer you get.

f Use your calculator to find the next six numbers in this pattern.

g Write down each answer you get.

h Copy and fill in:

These numbers are all multiples of …
Multiples of 5 end in … or …

Because 35 is a multiple of 5, 35 chairs will fit into an exact number
of stacks of 5.

2 Will 49 chairs fit into an exact number
of stacks of 7?

a Write down 7.

b On your calculator press   **7** **+** **+** **=**

c Write down the answer.

d Now press **=** again.

e Write down the answer you get.

f Use your calculator to find the next six numbers in this
pattern.

g Write down each answer you get.

h Is 49 a multiple of 7?

3 Use your calculator to work out the first ten multiples of 9.

a Write down 9.

b On your calculator press   **9** **+** **+** **=**

c Write down the answer you get.

d Use your calculator to find the next eight numbers in this
pattern.

 1, 2, 3

e Write down each answer you get.

3   Square and triangle numbers

Year 9 are having a year photograph taken.

Len Scap the photographer has stacked some PE benches for them to stand on.

If he has to add another row at the back, how many benches would there be in the fourth row?

How many benches are needed altogether?

Exercise 8:5

You will need some cubes for this exercise.

1 a Make the shape in Model 1.

   b How many cubes did you use?

Model 1

2 a Build Model 2 out of cubes.

   b How many cubes did you use?

Model 2

3 a Build Model 3 out of cubes.

   b How many cubes did you use?

Model 3

4 a Build Model 4 out of cubes.

 b How many cubes did you use?

Model 4

5 a Copy this table.

Model number	Number of cubes
1	1
2	3
3	6
4	10
5	
6	

 b Complete the table.
 You can build the models to help you.

Triangle numbers	The numbers in the second column

1 3 6 10 15 21 ...

are called **triangle numbers**.

You can build a triangular shape out of each of these numbers of cubes.

Exercise 8:6

Look at the differences between the triangle numbers.

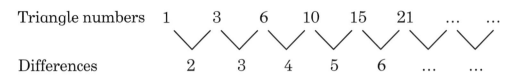

Triangle numbers   1   3   6   10   15   21   ...   ...

Differences   2   3   4   5   6   ...   ...

1   **a**   Write down the next two differences.

      b   What are the next two triangle numbers?

Square numbers

Two triangle numbers next to each other (consecutive) will fit together to make a square.

Use different coloured cubes.

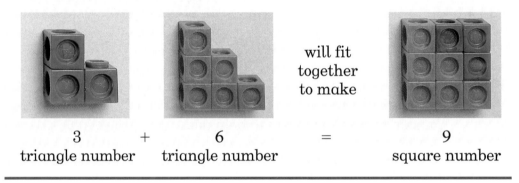

        3   +   6   will fit   =   9

triangle number   triangle number   together to make   square number

2   **a**   Make these models. Use different coloured cubes.

    1 cube      3 cubes

      b   Fit the two models together.
          They should make a square.

      c   How many cubes have you used altogether?

3 a Make a triangle using 6 cubes.

b Make a triangle using 10 cubes.
Use a different colour.

c Fit the two models together.
They should make a square.
Draw the square.

Write down the number of cubes
you have used.

Square numbers   1, 4, 9, 16 ...

are called **square numbers**.

You can build a square shape out of each
of these numbers of cubes.

You can find them by working out:

1 × 1 = 1   2 × 2 = 4   3 × 3 = 9   4 × 4 = 16

---

4 Copy and complete:

a 5 × 5 = ...   **c** 7 × 7 = ...   **e** 9 × 9 = ...

b 6 × 6 = ...   **d** 8 × 8 = ...   **f** 10 × 10 = ...

5 Write down the square numbers up to 100.

Factors of square numbers

Example

Arrange 9 counters in as many different rectangles as possible.
(Remember a square is a special rectangle.)

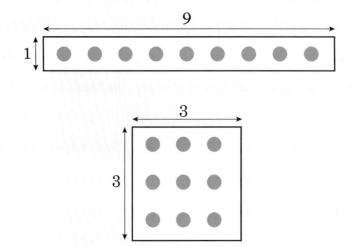
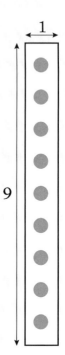

For 9 counters:

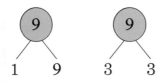

The factors of 9 are   1,   3,   9

Factors of 9 = {1,   3,   9}

---

6   Find the factors of these square numbers.

   a 4   **b** 16   **c** 25   **d** 36

H 6

1 Daniel is planting 18 bulbs in his garden .
He can plant them in three rows of 6, like this:

There must be the **same** number of bulbs in each row.

a Draw a diagram to show how he could plant the bulbs in two rows of 9.

b Draw a diagram to show a **different** way he can plant these 18 bulbs.

c Copy this table. Fill it in.

Number of rows	Number of bulbs in each row
1	
2	9
3	6
6	
9	
18	

d Sonya thinks she can plant 18 bulbs in 5 rows with the same number of bulbs in each row.
Explain why she is wrong.
You can draw a diagram.

2 a Write down the numbers that multiply together to give 24.

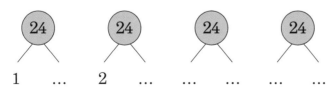

1 ... 2 ... ...

b Write down the factors of 24.

3 Copy and complete:

a Factors of 6 = {1, ..., ..., ...}

b Factors of 10 = {..., ..., ..., 10}

c Factors of 25 = {..., 5, ...}

d Factors of 12 = {..., ..., ..., ..., ..., ...}

4 The smallest prime number is 2.
Write down the next four prime numbers.

5 Write down the first five multiples of 4.

6 William draws a triangle using small squares.

Sarah draws a bigger triangle.

a How many small squares did William use?
b How many small squares did Sarah use?
c Draw the next triangle in the pattern?
d How many small squares are in this pattern?

7 Look at this list of numbers:
    4 7 9 13
a Write down the two prime numbers.
b Write down the two square numbers from the list.

9 Time

QUESTIONS

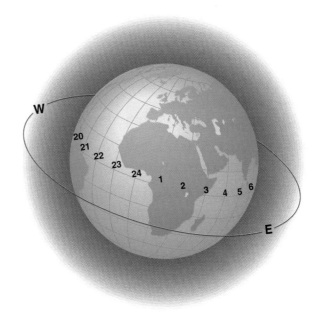

The basic unit of time measurement is the day. This is one rotation of the Earth on its axis. Dividing the day into hours and minutes and seconds is only for our convenience.

The second is defined in terms of the resonance vibration of the caesium-133 atom, as the interval occupied by 9 192 631 770 cycles.

1 Planning time

Rachel is planning a Year 9 disco for the end of term.
It will be on the last Friday in July.

She looks at the calendar to see what date that will be.

MAY						
M	...	3	10	17	24	31
T	...	4	11	18	25	...
W	...	5	12	19	26	...
T	...	6	13	20	27	...
F	...	7	14	21	28	...
S	1	8	15	22	29	...
S	2	9	16	23	30	...

JUNE					
M	...	7	14	21	28
T	1	8	15	22	29
W	2	9	16	23	30
T	3	10	17	24	...
F	4	11	18	25	...
S	5	12	19	26	...
S	6	13	20	27	...

JULY					
M	...	5	12	19	26
T	...	6	13	20	27
W	...	7	14	21	28
T	1	8	15	22	29
F	2	9	16	23	30
S	3	10	17	24	31
S	4	11	18	25	...

Exercise 9:1

1 Look at Rachel's calendar.

   a The letters M T W T F S S are at the side of each month.
   Write down what each letter stands for.

   b The last Friday in July is marked in red.
   What date is this?

2 Write down the days of the week for these dates.

   a 11th May   **b** 26th June   **c** 2nd July   **d** 30th May

3 **a** April is the month before May.
   What day of the week is 30th April?

   b What month comes after July?
   What day of the week is the 1st of this month?

1 ordinary year = 365 days
1 leap year = 366 days

Leap years are ..., 2000, 2004, 2008,
2012, 2016, ...

4 a How many years are there between leap years?

   b When is the next leap year after 2017?

5 The May Day holiday is on the first Monday in May.
What date is this?

6 School finishes for half-term on Friday 21st May.
The pupils have a full week's holiday then return to school the
next Monday.
What date will this be?

7 On the worksheet, shade in:

   a the May Day holiday

   b half-term

   c all Saturdays and Sundays.

   d School breaks up for the summer holidays on 23rd July.
   Shade in all days after this date.

The unshaded days are the days that pupils go to school in May,
June and July.

   e How many days is this?

To find the number of seconds in a minute, multiply the number of minutes by 60.

minutes → ×60 → seconds

To find the number of minutes in an hour, multiply the number of hours by 60.

hours → ×60 → minutes

To find the number of hours in a day, multiply the number of days by 24.

days → ×24 → hours

▼ H 1 *Exercise 9:2*

1 **a** How many seconds are there in one minute?
   b How many seconds are there in two minutes?
   c The sand takes three minutes to run through this egg timer. How many seconds is this?

2 **a** How many minutes are there in one hour?
   b How many minutes are there in two hours?
   c The Year 9 disco is from 8 pm to 11 pm. How many hours will the disco last?
   d How many minutes will the disco last?

3 Rachel has a 120 minute video tape. How many hours will the tape last?

4 **a** How many hours are there in one day?
   b How many hours are there in two days?
   c There are 72 hours before the disco. How many days is 72 hours?

5 **a** How many days are there in one week?
   b The school hall was booked four weeks before the disco. How many days are there in four weeks?

6 How many days are there in a year?

7 How many years are there in one century?

8 How many years in a millennium?

am	Times after midnight and up to noon are am.
pm	Times in the afternoon and evening are pm.

It is nearly time for the disco
The time is quarter past seven in the evening.
It can be written as 7.15 pm
Both are correct.

am and pm can also be shown on a time line

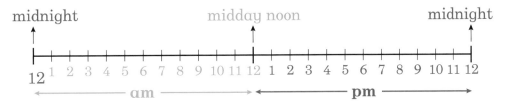

H 2 *Exercise 9:3*

1 Draw these times on clock faces.

   a Four o'clock.   **d** Quarter to five.

   b Quarter past four.   **e** Five o'clock.

   c Half past four.   **f** Quarter past five.

2 Write down the times shown on these clocks
   i in words
   ii in numbers with either am or pm.

a   **c**   **e**

b   **d**   **f**

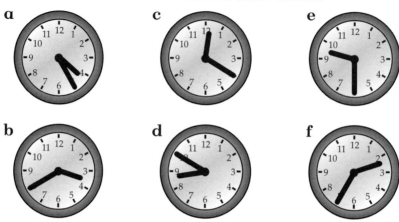

3 Write down the times on each of these clocks.

Sometimes we need a more accurate time.

The **hours** are shown by the numbers on a clock.
The short hand shows us the hour.

The **minutes** are shown by the long hand.
We count 5 minutes between each hour marked on the clock.

     7.00   2.10   4.25

4 **i**   **ii**   **iii**

  a Sharon has misread these three clocks.
    She says that the time on clock **i**   is 12.30
                            clock **ii** is 12.15
                            clock **iii** is 9.00
    Sharon is wrong.
    Write down the correct times on the clocks.

  b What mistake did Sharon make when she read the clocks?

3 **5** Draw these times on clock faces.
Write down if they are am or pm.
  a Ten past five in the morning.
  b Twenty past six in the evening.
  c Half past four in the afternoon.
  d Twenty-five past one in the morning.
  e Ten past nine in the evening.
  f Quarter past eleven in the morning.

Times can be shown on a clock face.

Time can be written in words, for example, quarter past five in the morning.

It can be written as am or pm   5.15 am

It can be written using 4 figures   05 : 15

1 **6** These things happened to Rachel on the day of the school disco.
Fill in the table.

What happened	am/pm	Time in words	Time using 4 figures
Woke up	...	Seven o'clock	07 : 00
Got up	7.30 am	...	...
Had breakfast	...	Eight o'clock	...
Phoned friends	...	Nine fifteen	...
Went by bus	9.40 am	...	...
Bought new jeans	...	Ten twenty	...
Walked home	...	Quarter past eleven	...
Washed hair	2.20 pm	...	14 : 20
Sorted CDs and tapes	...	Half past three	...
Got ready for disco	...	Twenty to seven	...
Arrived at disco	7.15 pm	Seven fifteen	...
Break for supper	...	Ten past nine	...
Help clear up	...	Ten to ten	...
Arrived home	11.40 pm	...	...

Time line There are 60 minutes in one hour.
Here is a time line to show the minutes in an hour,
at 5 minute intervals.

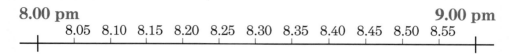

8.00 pm 8.05 8.10 8.15 8.20 8.25 8.30 8.35 8.40 8.45 8.50 8.55 **9.00 pm**

Lizzy puts some sausage rolls in
the oven at 8.30 pm.
They take 20 minutes to cook.
When will they be ready?

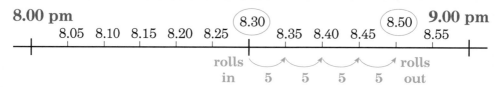

8.00 pm 8.05 8.10 8.15 8.20 8.25 (8.30) 8.35 8.40 8.45 (8.50) 8.55 **9.00 pm**

rolls in 5 5 5 5 rolls out

Mark 8.30 on the time line and count in 5s to 20.
You should have finished on 8.50.
The sausage rolls will be ready at 8.50 pm.

Exercise 9:4

 3 **1** Chicken pieces take 40 minutes to cook.
They go in the pan at 7.50 pm.
When will they be ready?

 3 **2** Work out the times when each of these will be cooked.

	Food to be cooked	Time put in oven	Time taken to cook	Take out time
a	Small cakes	3.10 pm	15 minutes	
b	Sponge cake	10.35 am	25 minutes	
c	Spareribs	7.10 pm	15 minutes	
d	Fruit pie	6.20 pm	45 minutes	
e	Pizza	4.45 pm	30 minutes	
f	Chocolate cake	10.20 am	50 minutes	

Rachel's mother is cooking a fruit cake.
She puts it in the oven at 9.30 am.
It will take 3 hours 30 minutes to cook.
When will it be ready?

We can use a time line.

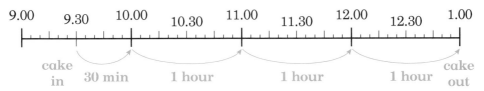

The cake will be ready at 1.00 pm.

W 3
G 1

3 Work out the times when each of these meals will be ready.
Use a time line.

	Food to be cooked	Time put in oven	Time taken to cook	Take out time
a	Sponge cakes	2.15 pm	1 h 15 min	
b	Treacle pudding	11.30 am	2 h 20 min	
c	Chicken curry	6.40 pm	1 h 35 min	
d	Roast potatoes	12.45 am	1 h 15 min	
e	Veggy bake	10.20 am	2 h 50 min	
f	Turkey	8.30 am	5 h 00 min	

W 4

4 Jaidee wants to cook beef curry.
It will take 2 hours 30 minutes.
She puts it in the oven at 10.30 am.
When will it be ready?

5 Liashan goes by train to London.
The journey lasts 2 hours 15 minutes.
She leaves Oxford at 5.30 pm.
When will she arrive in London?

6 Scott's new CD plays for 1 hour 20 minutes.
He starts to play it at 10.50 am.
When will it be finished?

2 Timetables

Alan lives in London.
His friend Sally lives near Parkway.
Alan is going to Sally's house.
He goes by train.
He looks at the train timetable.

Exercise 9:5

1 Look at this train timetable.

   a What time does the first train leave London?

   b What time does this train arrive in Parkway?

London depart	Parkway arrive
07:30	09:36
09:30	12:10
11:30	13:30
15:30	17:30
18:30	21:00

2 What time does the 11:30 from London arrive in Parkway?

3 A train arrives in Parkway at 17:30.
   What time did the train leave London?

4 Alan arrives at the station in London at 10:15.
   What time is the next train for Parkway?

5 a What time does the last train leave London for Parkway?

   b What time does this train arrive in Parkway?

Alan sees that the timetable uses the 24-hour clock.

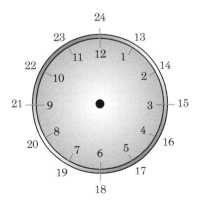

Take away 12 hours from the 24-hour clock times to get pm times.

Example

24-hour clock	am/pm
03:00	3 am
10:00	10 am
15:00	3 pm
23:00	11 pm

Remember.
24-hour clock
times ALWAYS
have 4 figures.

Exercise 9:6

1 Complete the time line on the worksheet.

2 Write these times as am or pm times.
Remember **am** is morning and **pm** is afternoon or evening.

   a 09:00   **c** 17:45   **e** 08:05   **g** 01:15
   b 17:00   **d** 21:00   **f** 23:15   **h** 13:15

Add 12 hours to pm times to get 24-hour clock times.

Example

am/pm	24-hour clock
8 pm	20:00
6.15 pm	18:15
4.25 am	04:25

Remember.
NEVER use
am or pm
with 24-hour
clock times.

3 Write these times using the 24-hour clock.

   a 4 pm   **c** 6 am   **e** 10.15 pm   **g** 1.40 am
   b 7 pm   **d** 11 am   **f** 3.26 pm   **h** 12.30 pm

4 Here is part of a bus timetable.
It shows when the bus arrives at a bus stop.

	1st bus	2nd bus	3rd bus	4th bus
Thornbury	07:00	08:00	16:00	17:00
Olveston	07:12	08:12	16:12	…
Little Stoke	07:50	08:50	…	17:50
Parkway Station	07:55	08:55	16:55	17:55

a When does the second bus leave Thornbury?

b When does the third bus leave Olveston?

c Where does the 16:00 from Thornbury **not stop**?

d The fourth bus does not stop at Olveston.
What time does it reach Parkway Station?

e How long is the journey from Thornbury to Parkway Station?

Jon arrives at Olveston at 07:50

f What time is the next bus?

g How long must he wait for the next bus?

Many timetables and machines use the 24-hour clock.

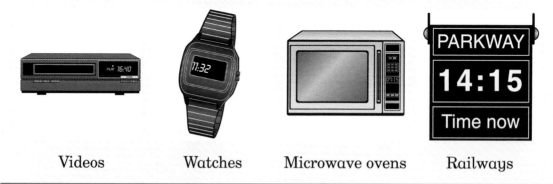

Videos   Watches   Microwave ovens   Railways

5 How many more examples can you think of?
Write them down.

There is another kind of time line.
It can help you to work out lengths of time.

Example   Wade sets the video from 09:30 to 11:20.
How long is the film that he records?

09:30   10:00   11:00   11:20

30 min   1 hour   20 min

The total time is   30 min + 1 hour + 20 min = 1 hour 50 min
The film is 1 hour 50 min long.

Exercise 9:7

 4

1 Owen sets his video from 16:45 to 18:10
How long is the program that he records?

2 Ayla puts the microwave oven on at 19:20.
It finishes at 20:05.
How long is it on?

3 When Sarah gets to the station, the clock reads 11:20.
The next train is at 13:30.
How long does she need to wait?

4 David's watch stopped at 12:35.
The real time is 15:30.
How long ago did his watch stop?

5 The coach leaves school at 08:50 and arrives at a theme
park at 11:55.
How long is the coach journey?

6 Look at this part of a timetable.

   a Work out how long each train takes.

   b Which is the quickest train?

London depart	Parkway arrive
14:30	16:40
16:15	18:30
17:40	19:45

Simon's Coaches travel from Bristol to London
each day in the summer.
This calendar shows when Simon's Coaches
run special services.

Simon's Summer Specials

MAY

M	T	W	T	F	S	S
1	2	3	4	5	6	7
8	9	10	11	12	13	14
15	16	17	18	19	20	21
22	23	24	25	26	27	28
29	30	31				

JUNE

M	T	W	T	F	S	S
			1	2	3	4
5	6	7	8	9	10	11
12	13	14	15	16	17	18
19	20	21	22	23	24	25
26	27	28	29	30		

JULY

M	T	W	T	F	S	S
					1	2
3	4	5	6	7	8	9
10	11	12	13	14	15	16
17	18	19	20	21	22	23
24	25	26	27	28	29	30
31						

AUGUST

M	T	W	T	F	S	S
	1	2	3	4	5	6
7	8	9	10	11	12	13
14	15	16	17	18	19	20
21	22	23	24	25	26	27
28	29	30	31			

Key: ■ special event day
midweek away day
■ short breaks

The table shows when Simon's Coaches depart (d) and arrive (a)
at London and Bristol

Bristol (d)	06:30	07:00	07:30	11:40	12:40	16:30
London (a)	09:30	10:00	10:30	15:00	16:00	19:00

London (d)	17:00	17:30	18:00	20:00	21:30	23:00
Bristol (a)	20:00	20:30	21:00	22:30	24:00	01:30

Exercise 9:8

Look at the calendar opposite.

1   How many days are there altogether in May, June, July and August?

2   How many weekends (Saturday/Sunday) are there?

Look at the key below the calendar

3   How is a Special Event Day shown on the calendar?

4   How many midweek away days are there? Write down their dates.

5   How many short breaks are there? Write down their dates.

Look at the timetable.

6   How many coaches travel to London each day?

The first coach gets to London at 09.30.

7   When does the second coach get to London?

8   How long does the second coach take to get to London?

9   How long does the 12:40 coach take?

10   How long does the 16:30 coach take?

11   I want to go to the Cup Final on May 13th. The match starts at 15:30.

    a   Is this a 'special event day'?

    b   What is the best coach to catch in Bristol to get to the match just in time.

    c   After the match I must be back in Bristol for 23:00. Which is the best return coach to catch?

12 The men's final at Wimbledon is July 9th.

    a What day of the week is this?

    230 people have booked with Simon's Coaches for July 9th.

    b If each coach carries 50 people, how many coaches will Simon need to take them to London?

£9 one way.
£12 day return
£38 short breaks

13 10 pupils from Year 9 book for a day return. How much will it cost?

14 110 pupils from Beaufort School visit the Millenium Dome. It costs £12 each. How much is this altogether?

15 Five students want to go on a short break to London. They can only go Thursday to Saturday in August.

    a What date can they go?

    b How much is the total cost?

1 Use the calendar opposite.

August						
M	...	2	9	16	23	30
T	...	3	10	17	24	31
W	...	4	11	18	25	...
Th	...	5	12	19	26	...
F	...	6	13	20	27	...
S	...	7	14	21	28	...
S	1	8	15	22	39	...

  a What is the date of the last Friday in August?

  b How many Mondays are there in August?

  c Write down the days of the week for these dates:

  i 26th August

  ii 1st August.

2 a How many minutes are there in one hour?

  b How many minutes are there in three hours?

  c Jon is having a party from 1 pm to 3 pm.

  i How many hours is the party?

  ii How many minutes is the party?

  iii How many seconds is the party?

Come to

Jon's Party

Saturday 28th
August 1pm-3pm

3 Write down the times shown on these clocks:

  i in words

  ii in numbers with am and pm.

a

afternoon

b

evening

c

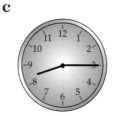

morning

4 Write these times using the 24-hour clock.

  a 9.30 am   **b** 7.15 pm   **c** 1.00 am   **d** 1.45 pm

5 Write these times using the 12-hour clock with am and pm.

  a 06:30   **b** 15:45   **c** 21:30   **d** 11:00

6   This is part of a bus timetable.

	Abingdon depart	**Oxford** arrive
Bus 1	14:10	15:10
Bus 2	16:20	17:00

a How long does each bus take?

b Which bus is quicker?

7   a A pizza takes 35 minutes to cook.
       Anton puts his pizza in the oven at 16:50.
       When will it be cooked?

   b A jacket potato takes 12 minutes to cook in a microwave.
       Ben puts his jacket potato in the microwave at 17:10.
       When will it be cooked?

10 Negative numbers

QUESTIONS

Under water, the deeper you go, the greater the weight and the *pressure* of water above you.

Nitrogen from an air supply is dissolved inside a diver's body under the high pressure.

If the diver comes back up too fast the nitrogen is released as tiny bubbles in the bloodstream. These bubbles can block the oxygen supply to tissues and organs causing dizziness and cramps – a condition known as 'the bends'.

1 Temperature

This is a picture of the planet Jupiter.
The average temperature on Jupiter is $-120\,°C$
Temperature is measured on the Celsius scale.

| **Negative numbers** | Numbers **below** 0 Numbers with a minus sign. |

Examples
$$-120$$
$$-50$$
$$-1$$

| **Positive numbers** | Numbers **higher** than 0 Can have a plus sign. |

Examples
$$3 \text{ or } +3$$
$$45 \text{ or } +45$$
$$100 \text{ or } +100$$

0 is not positive or negative

Exercise 10:1

1 From the list $-60, 10, 17, +35, 0, -43, -5$ write down
 a the negative numbers
 b the positive numbers
 c the number that is not positive or negative.

Number line

On a **number line** the numbers are written in order.

Example   This number line goes up in 1s, smallest number first. There are 3 numbers missing. Fill in the missing numbers.

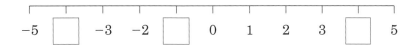

The missing numbers are −4, −1 and 4.
The number line should read

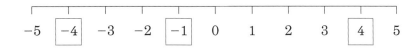

 2   Draw the number lines and fill in the missing numbers.
The number lines go up in 1s, smallest first.

a

b

Example   This number line goes up in 2s.
There are 2 missing numbers. Fill in the missing numbers.

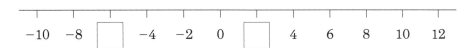

The missing numbers are −6 and 2.

 3   Write down the missing numbers for each line
The number lines go up in 2s, smallest first.

a
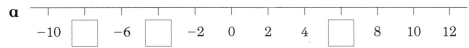

b

Example This number line goes up in 10s, smallest number first.
There are 3 missing numbers. Fill in the missing numbers.

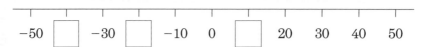

The missing numbers are −40, −20 and 10.
The number line should read

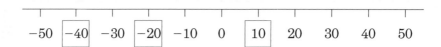

4 Draw the number line and fill in the missing numbers.
The number line goes up in 10s, smallest first.

a

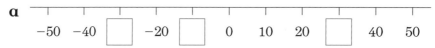

b

5 a Draw this number line.

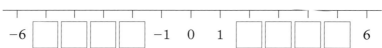

The line goes up in 1s.

b Finish labelling the line from −6 to 6.

6 a Draw this number line.

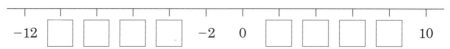

The line goes up in 2s.

b Label the line from −12 to 10. (Hint: start numbering from 0.)

7 a Draw this number line.

The line goes up in 10s.

b Label the line from −60 to 40.

Exercise 10:2

W1

1 On 1st January the temperature in Iceland was −20°C.
This is shown on a number line.

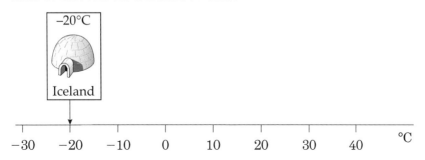

Cut out the pictures on the worksheet.
Stick them in the correct place, above or below the line.
Draw an arrow to mark the exact temperature.

a What was the temperature in   **i** Sydney
                                    ii Venice?
How much hotter was Sydney than Venice?

b What was the temperature in   **i** London
                                    ii Innsbruck?
How much colder was it in Innsbruck than London?

c Find the difference in temperature between the hottest and
the coldest place. (This is known as the **range**.)

2 In °C, temperatures lower than freezing are negative numbers.

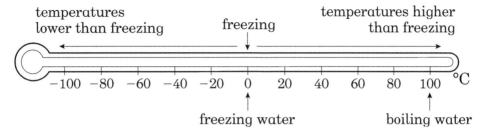

Look at the thermometer and write down
a the temperature in °C at which water freezes
b the temperature in °C at which water boils.

3 **a** **b** **c** **d** **e** **f**

a to f Write down the temperatures in °C shown on these thermometers.

Example Thermometer **a** shows 20 °C.

g Which thermometer shows the freezing point of water?

h How many of the temperatures shown are above freezing?

i Write down the temperatures that are below freezing.

j What is the hottest temperature shown?

k What is the coldest temperature shown?

l Write the temperatures in order starting with the coldest.

4

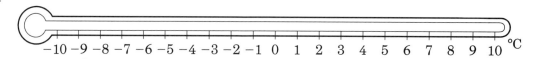

Put these temperatures in order, coldest first.

a −6 °C, 5 °C, −8 °C, 0 °C, 1 °C

b 3 °C, −1 °C, 4 °C, −2 °C, 10 °C

c −5 °C, 3 °C, −7 °C, 6 °C, −10 °C

<

means **'less than'**
(in temperature 'colder than')

>

means **'more than'**
(in temperature 'warmer than')

Example

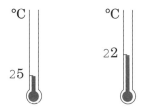

−5 °C	is **less than**	−2 °C
−5 °C	<	−2 °C
−5 °C is **colder than**		−2 °C

3 °C	is **more than**	−4 °C
3 °C	>	−4 °C
3 °C is **warmer than**		−4 °C

Exercise 10:3

1 a Look at these two thermometers.

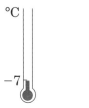 

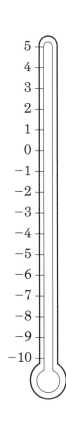

Copy and complete choosing
i 'less' or 'more'   −7 °C is ... than 1 °C.
ii sign **<** or **>**   −7 °C ... 1 °C.
iii 'colder' or 'warmer'   −7 °C is ... than 1 °C.

Fill in the spaces below as, in part **a**.

b i 6 °C	is ... than	−1 °C
ii 6 °C	...	−1 °C
iii 6 °C	is ... than	−1 °C

c i 4 °C	is ... than	0 °C
ii 4 °C	...	0 °C
iii 4 °C	is ... than	0 °C

d i −9 °C	is ... than	−5 °C
ii −9 °C	...	−5 °C
iii −9 °C	is ... than	−5 °C

e i 2 °C	is ... than	0 °C
ii 2 °C	...	0 °C
iii 2 °C	is ... than	0 °C

Temperatures rise and fall all the time.

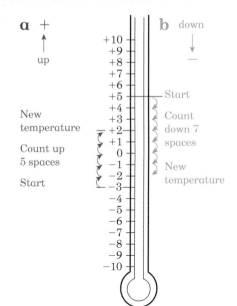

Examples

a Overnight the temperature is $-3\,°C$.
By morning it is $5\,°C$ warmer.
What is the temperature in the morning?

$$-3 + 5 = +2 \quad \text{(see diagram)}$$

In the morning the temperature is $2\,°C$.

b In the evening the temperature is $5\,°C$.
Overnight the temperature dropped by $7\,°C$.
What is the new temperature?

$$5 - 7 = -2 \quad \text{(see diagram)}$$

The new temperature is $-2\,°C$.

Exercise 10:4

 1 Complete the table.

Starting temperature	Temperature change	New temperature	
$-3\,°C$	$+5\,°C$	$2\,°C$	← Example **a**
$-2\,°C$	$+3\,°C$	...	
$3\,°C$	$+4\,°C$	...	
$-5\,°C$	$+2\,°C$	...	
$4\,°C$	$+4\,°C$	...	
$-1\,°C$	$+1\,°C$	...	
$-4\,°C$	$+3\,°C$	...	
$-2\,°C$	$+6\,°C$	...	

 2 Complete the table.

Starting temperature	Temperature change	New temperature	
$5\,°C$	$-7\,°C$	$-2\,°C$	← Example **b**
$8\,°C$	$-5\,°C$	...	
$4\,°C$	$-6\,°C$	...	
$6\,°C$	$-5\,°C$	...	
$2\,°C$	$-4\,°C$	...	
$0\,°C$	$-3\,°C$	...	
$-2\,°C$	$-5\,°C$	...	
$-1\,°C$	$-2\,°C$	...	

3 What is the difference between these day and night temperatures?
The first one has been done for you.

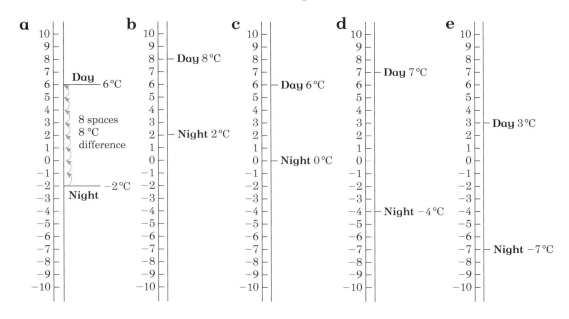

Activity

 5 You will need a Celsius thermometer.
Take the temperature indoors and outdoors at the times in the table.
Fill in the table.

Place	Time	Indoor temperature °C	Outdoor temperature °C
Home – morning			
School – morning			
School – midday			
School – afternoon			
Home – afternoon			
Home – night time			

a Arrange the indoor temperatures in order, coldest first.
What is the difference between the highest and lowest
temperatures (the **range**)?

b Arrange the outdoor temperatures in order, coldest first.
What is the **range** of outdoor temperatures in °C?

2　Other number scales

Temperature is not the only place where we use positive (+) and negative (−) numbers.

In a TV quiz game both teams start with 0 points.
Ken answers the first question.
He gets the answer wrong.
Ken's team **loses** 5 points.

0

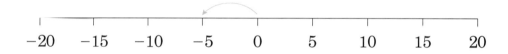

The score for Ken's team is now −5 points.

−5

Exercise 10:5

1　Use the number line for this question.

  a Ken's team gets the next two questions right.
    Their score goes **up** by 10 points.

$$-5 + 10 = \ldots$$

    What is their new score?

  b Gill's team goes down to −15 then gets a question right.

$$-15 + 5 = \ldots$$

    What is their new score?

2 In the lift at Read's shop there is a guide to help you find which floor you need.

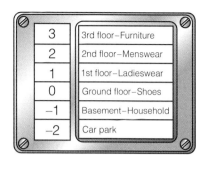

3	3rd floor–Furniture
2	2nd floor–Menswear
1	1st floor–Ladieswear
0	Ground floor–Shoes
−1	Basement–Household
−2	Car park

   a What number is used for the ground floor?

   b On which floor do you find Ladieswear?

   c Where do you go if you press −2?

   d Katie goes from the Basement to the 3rd floor.
   How many floors does she go up?

   e The manager goes from Menswear to Ladieswear?
   How many floors does he go down?

   f If you leave your car in the Car Park and want to look at furniture, how many floors do you go up?

3 Numbers above sea level are positive.
Numbers below sea level are negative.
Look at the metre scale on the diagram.

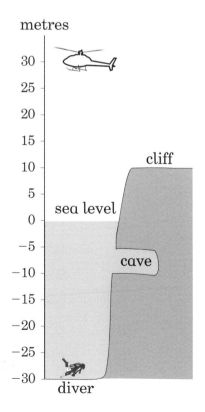

   a At what number is sea level?

   b At what height above sea level is the helicopter?

   c How high above sea level is the top of the cliff?

   d How many metres higher than the top of the cliff is the helicopter?

   e The diver is looking at the sea bed. How many metres below sea level is the sea bed?

   f How many metres below sea level is the bottom of the cave?

   g How many metres must the diver swim up to enter the cave?

Bank accounts

Balance	The **balance** is the amount of money you have in your account *or* the money you owe the bank.
Overdrawn	You are **overdrawn** when you owe the bank money. This happens when the balance is a negative number.
Paid in	Money or cheques **paid in** are **added** to your balance.
Taken out	Money or cheques **taken out** are **subtracted** from your balance.

4 Calculate the **new** balance after the following amounts have been paid in or taken out.
The first three have been done for you.

	Old balance	Taken out −	Paid in +	New balance (write + or −)
a	£100	£60		£100 − £60 = +£40
b	£15		£20	£15 + £20 = +£35
c	£20	£30		£20 − £30 = −£10
d	£50		£30	...
e	£60	£20		...
f	£25	£15		...
g	£10	£30		...
h	−£10		£20	...

G 2

1   From the list $-15, 7, +12, -6, 0, 20, -3$ write down

   a the negative numbers

   b the positive numbers

   c the number that is not positive or negative.

2   Draw the number lines and fill in the missing numbers.

   a This number line goes up in 1s.

   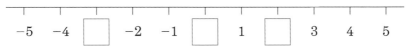

   b This number line goes up in 2s.

   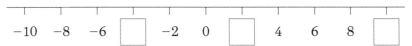

   c This number line goes up in 10s.

   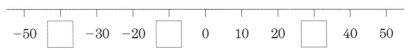

   d This number line goes up in 2s.

3   Write down the temperatures in °C shown on these thermometers.

   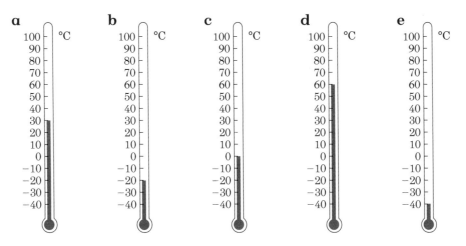

   f Put the temperatures **a** to **e** in order, coldest first.

4 **<** is less than
> is more than

   a Write down if the statements below are **true** or **false**.

     i $3\,°C < 8\,°C$ **ii** $1\,°C > 4\,°C$ **iii** $-1\,°C > 4\,°C$

   b Put the correct sign $<$ or $>$ between each pair of numbers.

     i $6 \ldots -2$ **ii** $-10 \ldots 5$ **iii** $-7 \ldots -2$

5 Complete the table.

Starting temperature	Temperature change	New temperature
$-4\,°C$	$+3\,°C$	...
$-2\,°C$	$+5\,°C$	...
$-8\,°C$	$+8\,°C$	...
$7\,°C$	$-5\,°C$	...
$3\,°C$	$-6\,°C$	...
$-4\,°C$	$-5\,°C$	...

6 In the picture:

   a How far below sea level is the jellyfish?

   b How many metres above the bottom of the sea is the jellyfish?

   c How far above sea level is the seagull?

   d How many metres above the bottom of the sea is the seagull?

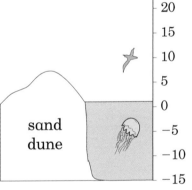

7 Calculate the **new** balance after the following amounts have been paid in or taken out.

	Old balance	Taken out	Paid in	New balance
a	£50	£20		...
b	£10		£30	...
c	£40	£40		...
d	£20	£30		...
e	−£10		£20	...

11 Statistics: above average

QUESTIONS

High jump

Javelin

100 metres sprint

How many different sports take place at your sports day?

1 Sports Day averages

This is the 100 metre final on Sports Day.

What makes a good runner?

What is the average runner like?

Averages are used to compare data.
The values are added up and shared out to find
the mean average.

Mean   To find the **mean**
add up all the values then divide by the number of values.

Example   Here are the heights of 4 runners:

   153 cm   156 cm   154 cm   157 cm

Find the mean height of the
4 runners.

To find the mean height,
add the heights

   153 cm + 156 cm + 154 cm + 157 cm = 620 cm

then divide by 4 because there are 4 runners

   620 cm ÷ 4 = 155 cm

The mean height is 155 cm

Exercise 11:1

You need a calculator for these questions.

1 Boys' 200 metres race.

161 cm   158 cm   160 cm   161 cm

a Find the total of the heights.

b What number do you divide by to calculate the mean?

c Find the mean height of the runners.

2 Girls' 400 metres race.

151 cm   153 cm   155 cm   152 cm   159 cm

a Find the total of the heights.

b What number do you divide by to calculate the mean?

c Find the mean height of the runners.

3 Boys' 400 metres race.

159 cm   156 cm   157 cm   161 cm   162 cm

a Find the total of the heights.

b What number do you divide by to calculate the mean?

c Find the mean height of the runners.

4 Girls' 100 metres race.

149 cm   152 cm   152 cm
151 cm   148 cm   160 cm

a Find the total of the heights.

b What number do you divide by to calculate the mean?

c Find the mean height of the runners.

5 These are some Year 7 long jump results:

3.3 m   2.9 m   3.4 m   3.0 m   3.1 m
3.4 m   3.1 m   3.5 m   3.1 m

a Find the total of the lengths.

b What number do you divide by to calculate the mean?

c Find the mean length of the Year 7 long jumps.

6 Here are some Year 8 long jump results:

3.8 m   3.5 m   3.7 m   4.2 m   4.1 m
3.9 m   4.1 m   3.7 m   4.1 m

a Find the total of the lengths.

b What number do you divide by to calculate the mean?

c Find the mean length of the Year 8 long jumps.

7 These are some Year 9
long jump results:

4.0 m   4.6 m   4.8 m   3.9 m
3.8 m   4.2 m   4.8 m

a Find the total of the lengths.

b What number do you divide by
to calculate the mean?

c Find the mean length of the Year 9 long jumps.

8 Measure the height of 5 people
in your class.
Find the mean height of the
5 people.

a Find the total of the heights.

b What number do you divide
by to calculate the mean?

c Find the mean height.

The Olympic Games is held every 4 years in different countries around the world.

Competitors can win bronze, silver or gold medals.

Exercise 11:2

This table shows all the gold, silver and bonze medals won by the USA in 3 different Olympic Games.

Year	Gold	Silver	Bronze
1996	42	32	25
1992	37	33	37
1988	35	31	27

1 **a** How many gold medals did the USA win in 1992?

   b How many bronze medals did they win in 1988?

   c How many silver medals did they win in 1992?

   d How many gold medals did they win in 1996?

   e How many silver medals did they win in 1988?

2 **a** In which year did they win the most bronze medals?

   b In which year did they win the most gold medals?

3 **a** How many medals did they win in total in 1996?

   b How many medals did they win in total in 1992?

   c How many medals did they win in total in 1988?

   d In which year did they win the most medals altogether?

4 **a** Find the mean number of gold medals won.
         Write down your calculation.

   b Find the mean number of silver medals won.
         Write down your calculation.

   c Find the mean number of bronze medals won.
         Write down your calculation.

| Mode | Another type of average is the **mode**
The mode is easy to find.
The **mode** is the **most common** or **most popular value.** |

Example

These are the distances thrown in a javelin competition.
The values are to the nearest metre.
Find the mode.

90 m   90 m   95 m   91 m   89 m   84 m   90 m

It is easier to see the most common value if you rewrite the values in order, smallest first.

84 m   89 m   **90 m**   **90 m**   **90 m**   91 m   95 m

The modal distance is **90 m**.

The **mode** is 90 m. It is the **most common value.**

Exercise 11:3

1   These are the results from some other javelin competitions.

Rewrite the values in order.
Find the mode for each competition.

a 89 m   90 m   88 m   90 m   86 m   84 m   87 m

b 87 m   84 m   87 m   87 m   84 m   83 m   83 m

c 85 m   82 m   85 m   88 m   85 m   87 m   89 m

d 86 m   88 m   89 m   88 m   88 m   87 m   86 m

2   Anish asked some spectators which was their favourite event.
Write down the modal answer for each group.

a Javelin   Discus   Javelin   Javelin   Discus   Shot putt
Javelin

b 100 m   200 m   200 m   400 m   800 m   200 m   800 m
100 m   200 m

c High jump   Long jump   High jump   Triple jump
High jump

3 This table shows some results for the women's javelin in the Olympic Games.
The distances have been rounded to the nearest metre.

Year	Gold	Silver	Bronze
1968	60	60	58
1972	64	63	60
1976	66	65	64
1980	68	68	67
1984	70	69	67
1988	75	70	67
1992	68	68	67

a How far was the winning throw in 1968?

b How far was the winning throw in 1984?

c Which year had the longest winning throw?

d Which year had the shortest winning throw?

e Find the mode for gold.

f Find the mode for silver.

g Find the mode for bronze.

4 There can be more than one mode.

Ask 8 people in your class this question:

"What is your favourite sport?"

Write down their answers.
Write down the mode answer.

Median   The **median** is another type of average.
The **median** is the **middle value** when the data values are written in order.
Put all the data in order, smallest first.
Find the middle number.
This is the median.

Example

Fiona plays hockey.

These are the number of goals she scored over a season.

4 1 0 3 2 4 2 1 0

Put the values in order, smallest first.

0 0 1 1 ② 2 3 4 4

The middle number is **2**

The **median** value is **2**.

Exercise 11:4

1 Matthew plays waterpolo.

These are the number of goals he scored over a season.

3 2 0 1 3 4 3

a Write the numbers in order, smallest first.

b Find the middle number.

c Write the sentence
'The median number of goals scored by Matthew was …'
and fill in the answer.

2 Joanne plays netball:

These are the number of goals she scored over a season.

6 3 0 5 5 2 1 5 8 2 4

a Write the numbers in order, smallest first.

b Find the middle number.

c Write the sentence
'The median number of goals scored by Joanne was …'
and fill in the answer.

3 Toby plays football.

These are the number of goals he scored over a season.

2 0 1 0 1 2 3 0 1 1 0

a Write the numbers in order, smallest first.

b Find the middle number.

c Write the sentence
'The median number of goals scored by Toby was …'
and fill in the answer.

4 Jenny plays basketball.

These are the number of baskets she scored in one season.

20 31 19 22 32 51
15 27 49 28 46

a Write the numbers in order, smallest first.

b Find the middle number.

c Write the sentence
'The median number of baskets scored by Jenny was …'
and fill in the answer.

If there are an even number of data values you can't find the middle number.

Example   Sally plays football

These are the number of goals she scored over a season.

2 1 0 3 1 2 3 1 0 2

Write the numbers in order, smallest first

0 0 1 1 ① ② 2 2 3 3

The median is the mean of these two numbers.

Find the mean: $\dfrac{1+2}{2} = 1.5$

The median is **1.5** goals.

---

5 Simon plays rugby.
These are the points Simon scored
over a season.

21 3 0 24 18 19 23 17

a Write the numbers in order,
smallest first.

b Find the middle values.

c Find the median.

d Write this sentence
'The median number of points scored by Simon is …'
and fill in the answer.

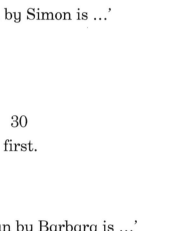

6 Barbara is training to run a marathon.
She records the number of kilometres
she runs each day she is training.

15 21 23 18 24 35 28 37 42 30

a Write the numbers in order, smallest first.

b Find the middle values.

c Find the median.

d Write the sentence
'The median number of kilometres run by Barbara is …'
and fill in the answer.

7 Chris goes swimming regularly.
He records the number of lengths
he swims each time

22 12 18 32 42 34 20 40 38 36

a Write the numbers in order,
smallest first.

b Find the middle values.

c Find the median.

d Write this sentence
'The median number of lengths swum by Chris was …'
and fill in the answer.

8 Roy finds the shoe sizes of 10 people in his class

3 8 6 5 7 6 5 4 7 8

a Write the numbers in order, smallest first.

c Find the median.

d Write this sentence
'The median shoe size in Roy's class is …'
and fill in the answer.

2 Solving problems with statistics

These two classes are taking the same maths test.

Both classes have the same mean average mark.

9Ks highest mark is 80 and lowest mark is 20.
9Ms highest mark is 60 and lowest mark is 40.

The difference between the highest and lowest mark is called the **range**.
9K and 9M have a different range.

Range   The **range** of a set of data values is the highest value take away the lowest value.

Example   Ruth's class take a maths test. These are the results:

   23   19   17   25   19   28   23   25   26

The highest mark is **28**.
The lowest mark is 17.
The range is   **28** – 17.
The range is 11.

Exercise 11:5

1 Some pupils in 9F took a maths test. Here are the results:

   15   12   17   16   19   15   16   17   14

   a How many pupils took the test?

   b What is the highest mark?

   c What is the lowest mark?

   d What is the range of marks?

2 Some pupils in 9T took a spelling test. Here are the results:

9 18 10 19 15 12 10 17

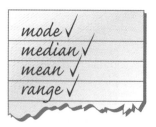

a How many pupils took the test?

b What is the highest mark?

c What is the lowest mark?

d What is the range of marks?

mode ✓
median ✓
mean ✓
range ✓

3 Some pupils in 9A took a science test. Here are the results:

72 66 51 79 88 53 67 82 85

a How many pupils took the test?

b What is the highest mark?

c What is the lowest mark?

d What is the range of marks?

4 Some pupils in 9S took a geography test. Here are the results:

78 83 67 79 66 98 77 67 66

a How many pupils took the test?

b What is the highest mark?

c What is the lowest mark?

d What is the range of marks?

5 Some pupils in 9N took a history test. Here are the results:

54 54 55 52 56 57 51 54 56 55

a How many pupils took the test?

b What is the highest mark?

c What is the lowest mark?

d What is the range of marks?

The range can help you compare two sets of data values.

Example Toby and Matt both play cricket.

These are their results for the last 5 matches.

Toby	50	35	40	50	75
Matt	100	5	45	40	60

Toby's mean score is $\dfrac{50 + 35 + 40 + 50 + 75}{5} = 50$ runs

Toby's range is $75 - 35 = 40$

Matt's mean score is $\dfrac{100 + 5 + 45 + 40 + 60}{5} = 50$ runs

Matt's range is $100 - 5 = 95$

Both boys have the same mean.
Toby's range is lower.
Toby's batting is more consistent.

Exercise 11:6

 1

These questions use data that was collected from 10 pupils when they were in Year 9 and now they are in Year 11. The data is on Data Sheet 1.

1 **a** How many girls were chosen?

    b How many boys were chosen?

2 **a** What is the height of Pupil 1 in Year 9?

    b What is the height of Pupil 6 in Year 9?

3 **a** What is the total of the Year 9 **boys'** heights?

    b What is the **mean** height of the Year 9 boys?

    c What is the **range** of the Year 9 boys' heights?

4 **a** What is the total of the Year 9 **girls'** heights?

    b What is the **mean** height of the Year 9 girls?

    c What is the **range** of the Year 9 girls' heights?

5 In Year 9, who were the tallest, on average, the boys or the girls?

6 **a** What is the height of Pupil 1 in Year 11?

    b What is the height of Pupil 6 in Year 11?

7 **a** What is the total of the Year 11 **boys'** heights?

    b What is the **mean** height of the Year 11 boys?

    c What is the **range** of the Year 11 boys' heights?

8 **a** What is the total of the Year 11 **girls'** heights?

   b What is the **mean** height of the Year 11 girls?

   c What is the **range** of the Year 11 girls' heights?

9 In Year 11, who were the tallest, on average, the boys or the girls?

Exercise 11:7

You will need Data Sheet 1 for this exercise too.

 1

1 Look at the shoe sizes of Year 9 boys.

   a Write them in order, smallest first.

   b Write down the median shoe size.

   c Write down the modal shoe size.

   d Write down the range.

2 Look at the shoe sizes of Year 9 girls.

   a Write them in order, smallest first.

   b Write down the median shoe size.

   c Write down the modal shoe size.

   d Write down the range.

3 Write two sentences to compare the Year 9 shoe sizes for boys and girls. Use your answers to questions **1** and **2**.

4 Look at the shoe sizes of Year 11 boys.

   a Write them in order, smallest first.

   b Write down the median shoe size.

   c Write down the modal shoe size.

   d Write down the range.

5 Look at the shoe sizes of Year 11 girls.

   a Write them in order, smallest first.

   b Write down the median shoe size.

   c Write down the modal shoe size.

   d Write down the range.

6 Write two sentences to compare the Year 11 shoe sizes for boys and girls. Use your answers to questions **4** and **5**.

Exercise 11:8

My class

You will need the Data Collection Sheet for this exercise, or draw one of your own.

1. Choose 10 people in your class.
   You can be one of them!

2. Measure each person's arm length. Write the lengths on the sheet.

3. Write down each person's shoe size on the sheet.

4. Choose two other items of data about the pupils to collect.

5. For each set of data:
   • Find the mean.
   • Find the mode.
   • Find the median.
   • Find the range.

6. Write a report about what you found out.
   Include as much information as possible.

1 These are the heights of 5 boys:

  134 cm   160 cm   138 cm   150 cm   138 cm

a Find the total of the heights.

b Find the mean height of the 5 boys.

2 These are the heights of 7 girls:

  152 cm   140 cm   138 cm   152 cm
  160 cm   147 cm   144 cm

a List the heights in order, smallest first.

b Find the median height.

c Find the mode.

d Which is the greatest height?

e Which is the lowest height?

f What is the range of heights?

3 These are the numbers of awards received by six Year 9 tutor groups:

  32   40   32   35   60   50

a List the numbers of awards in order, smallest first.

b Find the median number of awards received.

c Find the mode.

d What is the highest number of awards received?

e What is the lowest number of awards received?

f What is the range?

4 The table shows some data collected from ten Year 9 pupils.

Shoe size	5	8	3	5	8	4	3	4	5	6
Height (cm)	160	161	170	152	150	130	152	158	164	173
Brothers/sisters	2	0	2	4	3	1	2	3	2	1

Find the mean, mode, median and range for:

a shoe size

b height

c number of brothers and sisters.

12 Try angles

QUESTIONS

These satellite dishes are set at a precise angle of elevation and direction (east) to receive TV broadcasts from a satellite orbiting the Earth. Find out what the angle is.

1 Turning through angles

Steve tries to steer his surfboard in a straight line.

He knows that if the front of his surfboard turns to the left or the right then it has made an angle with the straight line.

The angle of the turn may be **clockwise** or **anticlockwise**.

anticlockwise

clockwise

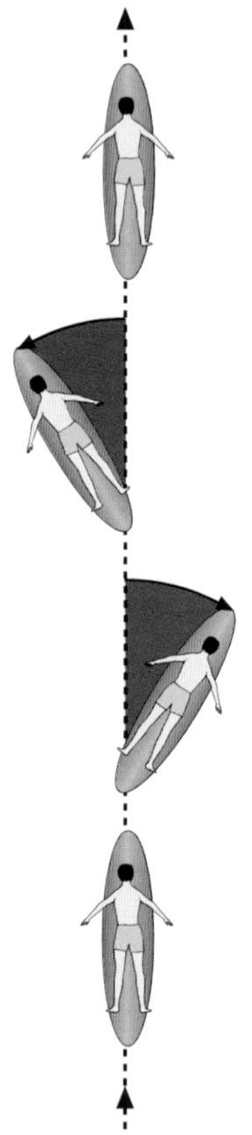

Exercise 12:1

1 Write down for each turn either clockwise or anticlockwise.

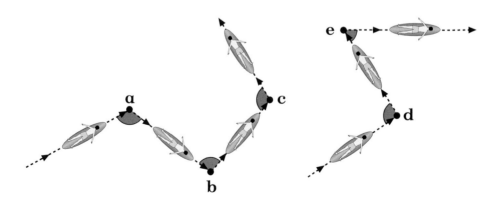

Compass directions   A compass can be used to show the direction of a turn.

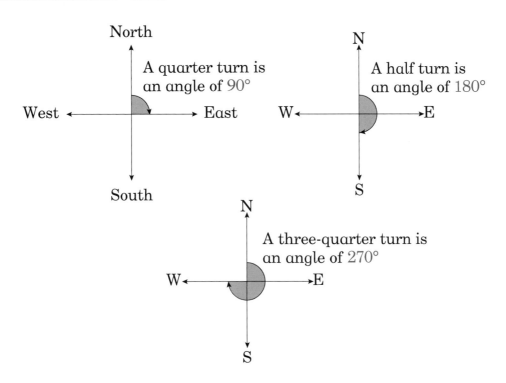

North

A quarter turn is an angle of 90°

West ← → East

South

N

A half turn is an angle of 180°

W ← → E

S

N

A three-quarter turn is an angle of 270°

W ← → E

S

Examples

1   This canoe is going north. What direction and angle will it go if it turns a quarter turn anticlockwise?

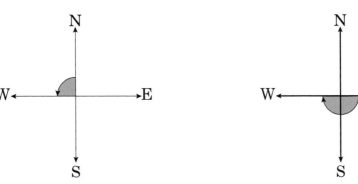

N

N

W ← → E

S

Answer   West 90°

2   This canoe is going east.

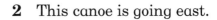 → E

What direction and angle will it go if it turns a half turn clockwise?

N

W ← → E

S

Answer   West 180°

2 Copy and complete this table. The first one is already done.

	Start direction	Turn	New direction	Angle turned
a	North	Half turn anticlockwise	South	180°
b	East	Quarter turn anticlockwise		
c	South	Three-quarter turn clockwise		
d	West	Half turn clockwise		
e	North	Three-quarter turn anticlockwise		

Right angle $\frac{1}{4}$ turn is called a **right angle**.

The corners of squares and rectangles are right angles.

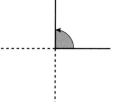

A right angle is often shown like this:

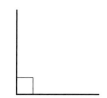

$\frac{1}{2}$ turn makes a straight angle or line.

A full turn makes a complete circle.

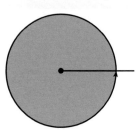

Exercise 12:2

1 a Draw these rectangles

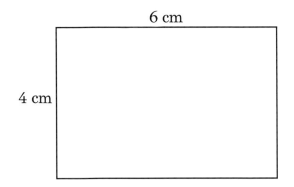

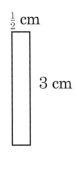

b Mark the corners using the sign for a right angle.

| **Degrees** | We use **degrees** (written °) to measure angles. |

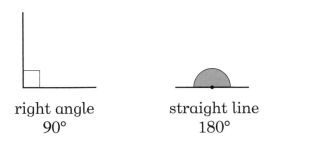

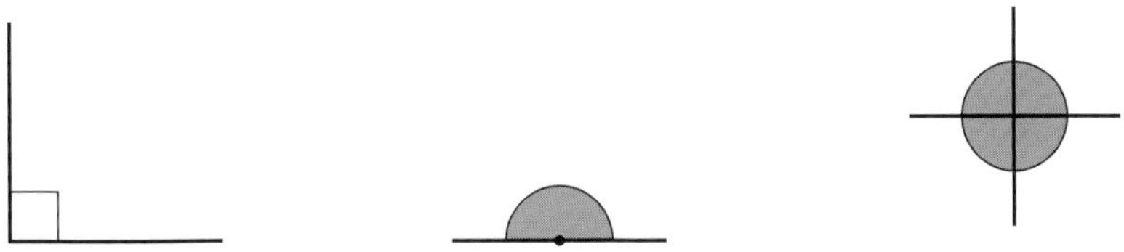

right angle   straight line   full turn
90°   180°   360°

Acute Obtuse Reflex

Acute angle   Obtuse angle   Reflex angle

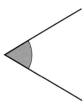

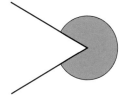

less than 90°   between 90° and 180°   between 180° and 360°

2 Fill in Worksheet 2.

213

It is useful to estimate the size of an angle in degrees.

Exercise 12:3

1 Take a piece of tracing paper.

   a Fold it to make a straight line.

   b Fold it again to make a right angle, 90°.

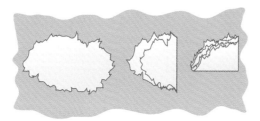

2 Take another piece of tracing paper.

   a Fold it to make a straight line.

   b Fold it again to make a right angle.

   c Fold it again to make an angle of 45°

Example   Estimate the sizes of these angles.

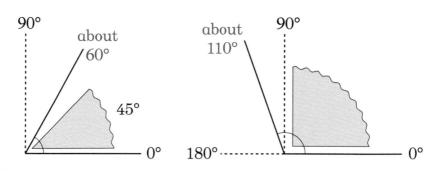

---

3 For each of the angles opposite, say if it is **acute**, a **right angle** or **obtuse**.
Then estimate the size in degrees to the nearest 5°.
Use your folded right angle and 45° angle to help you.

Copy the table and fill in your answers.
You will need the 'Actual' column later.

	Name	Estimate	Actual
a			
b			
c			
d			
e			
f			
g			
h			

a

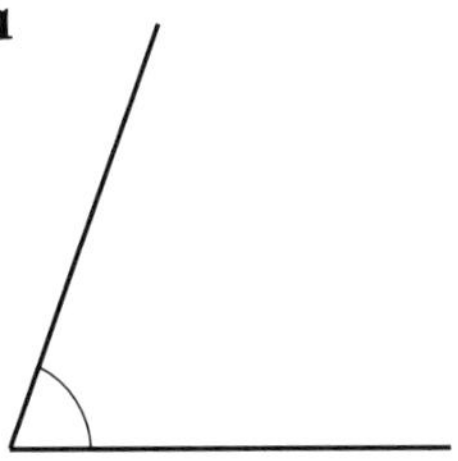

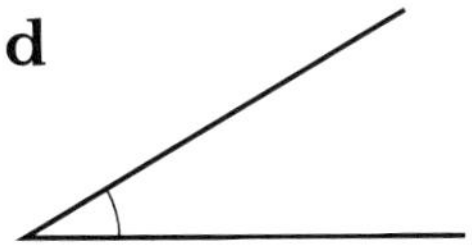

e

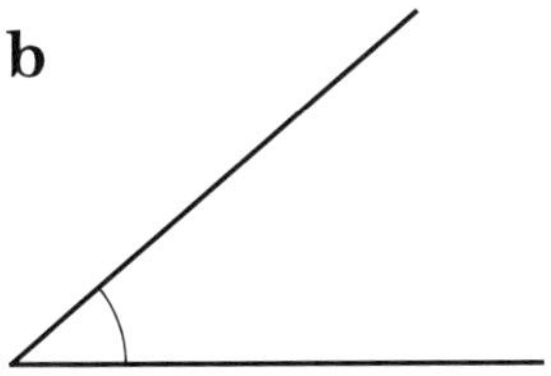

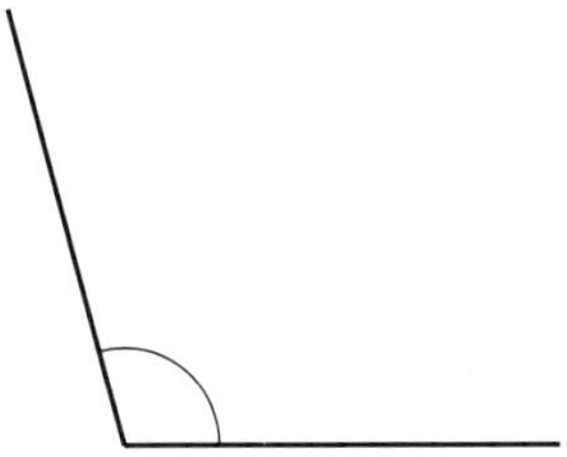

b

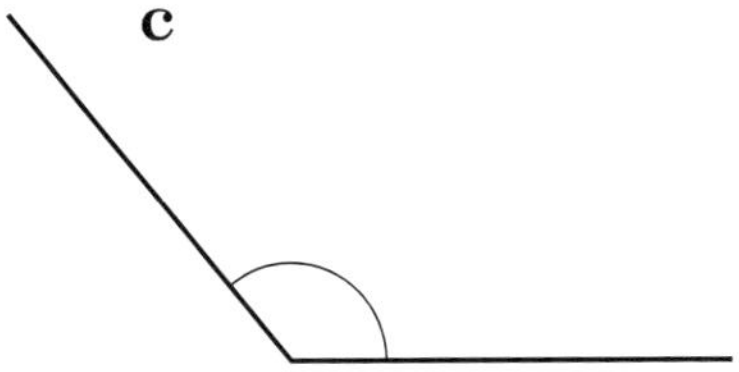

f

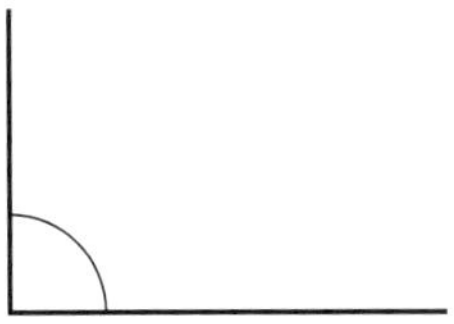

c

g

d

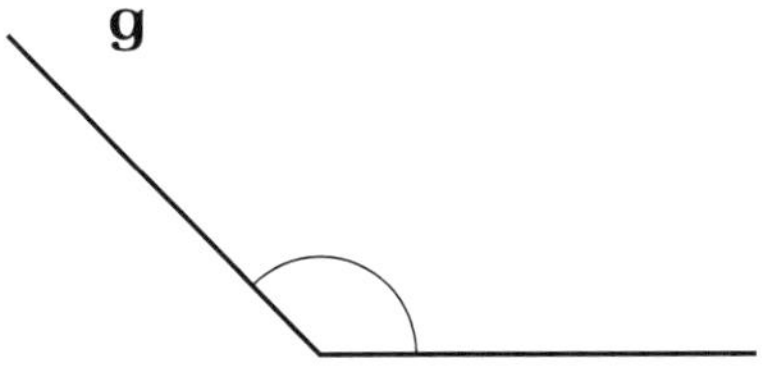

h

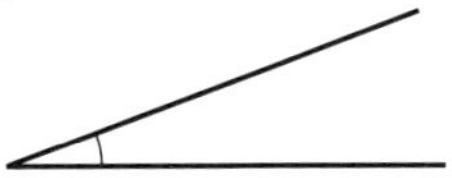

W 3, 4   **4**   Drop the angles into the correct buckets on Worksheets 3 and 4.

Measuring and drawing angles

We can use an angle measurer or a protractor to measure angles.

They both have two scales. One is clockwise. The other is anticlockwise.

Example   Using an angle measurer to measure an angle.

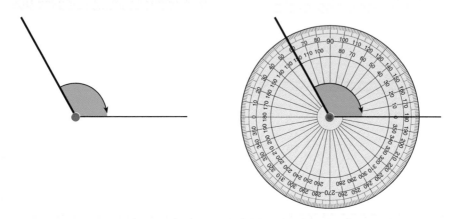

Make sure that the 0° line covers the dark arm of the angle.
The mid point must be placed on the point of the angle.
Now count round in 10s from zero. The angle is 120°.

Example   Using a protractor to measure an angle.

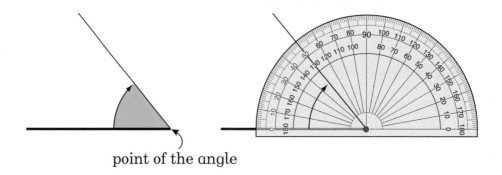

point of the angle

Make sure that the 0° line covers the dark arm of the angle.
The mid point must be placed on the point of the angle.
Now count round in 10s from zero. The angle is 60°.

---

5   Use your angle measurer or protractor to measure the angles in question **3**.
Write your answers in the 'Actual' column of your table.

Drawing angles with an angle measurer or protractor

To draw an angle of 60°:

(1) Draw a line about 8 cm long.	(2) Place the angle measurer with the centre on the end point of the line. Make sure that the 'bold' zero line of the angle measurer lies along your line. 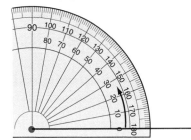
(3) Follow the arrow that points up 0 → 10 → 20 ... → 60. Put a little pencil mark on your paper at 60. 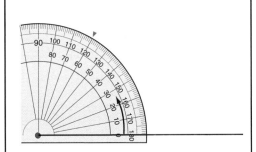	(4) 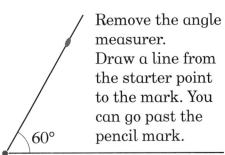 Remove the angle measurer. Draw a line from the starter point to the mark. You can go past the pencil mark. 60° Label the angle like this.

Exercise 12:4

1 Use your angle measurer to draw these angles.
Label each angle.

a 60°	**d** 45°	**g** 135°
b 80°	**e** 90°	**h** 150°
c 30°	**f** 120°	**i** 170°

 5   **2** Follow the worksheet to find out an important fact about 'angles on a straight line'.

2   Calculating with angles

We do not always find angles by **measuring**.

We can calculate angles.
We do not need to use an angle measurer.

None of the diagrams in this section are drawn accurately.
Calculate the angles instead of measuring.

The angles on a straight line add up to 180°.

Example   Calculate angle *a*.

$a = 180° - 80°$

$a = 100°$

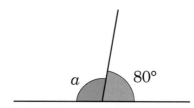

Exercise 12:5

1   Calculate angle *a*.

Show your working like this:
$a = 180° - 40°$
$a = ...$

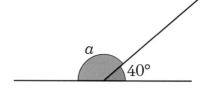

2   Calculate the angles marked with letters.

a

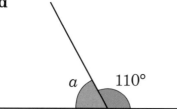

b

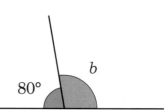

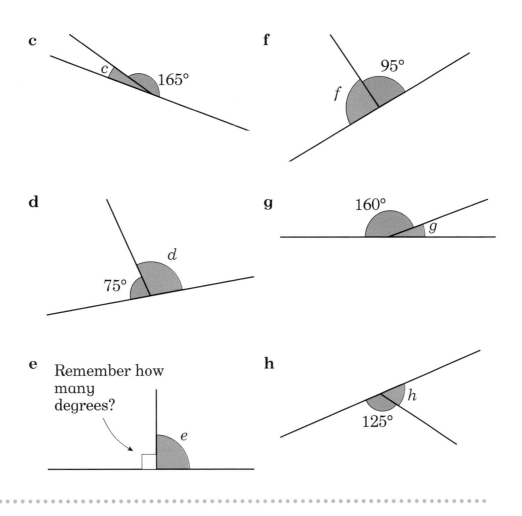

c 165° c

f 95° f

d 75° d

g 160° g

e Remember how many degrees? e

h 125° h

The angles at a point make a full turn.
They add up to 360°.

Examples

a Find the size of angle *a*.

Show the working like this:

$a = 360° - 290°$
$a = 70°$

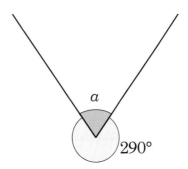

a 290°

b Find the size of angle b.

Show the working like this:

$b = 360° - 300°$
$b = 60°$

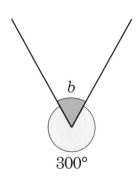

$300°$

Exercise 12:6

1 Calculate the angles marked with letters.

a

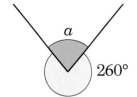

$260°$

e

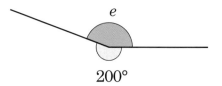

$200°$

b

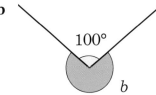

$100°$

f

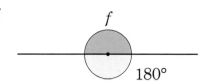

$180°$

c

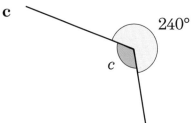

$240°$

g

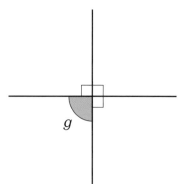

d

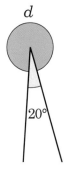

$20°$

h

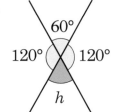

$60°$

$120°$ $120°$

h

Opposite angles are equal

Examples

1 Find the angles marked with letters.

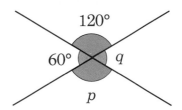

p is opposite 120°
q is opposite 60°
p = 120°   q = 60°

2 Find the angle marked with letter a.

Write your answer like this:

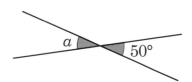

a is opposite 50°
a = 50°

Exercise 12:7

1 Find the angles marked with letters.

a

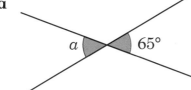

d

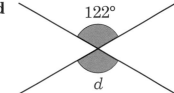

b

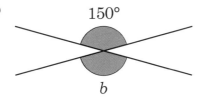

e

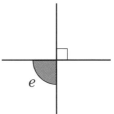

c

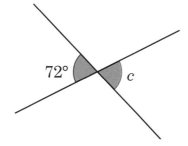

f

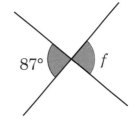

6   **2** **a** Draw a triangle.
Make each side at least 6 cm long.

b Measure each angle of the triangle.
Label each angle with its size.

c Add the 3 angles together.
Write down the answer inside your triangle.

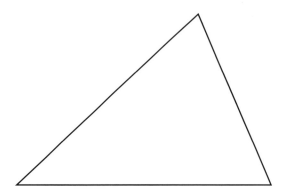

d Draw 2 more triangles.
Measure their angles.
Add the 3 angles together.

e What do you notice about the answers to parts **c** and **d**?

3 Angles in triangles

Sometimes you need to calculate an angle in a triangle.

You can use a calculator.

The angles of a triangle add up to 180°.

Example Calculate angle *a*.

Show your working like this:

$a = 180° - 85° - 65°$
$a = 30°$

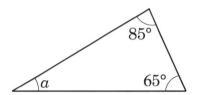

Exercise 12:8

1 Calculate the size of angle *a*.

Show your working like this:
$a = 180° - 100° - 50° =$

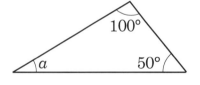

If you use a calculator key in:

1 8 0 − 1 0 0 − 5 0 =

2 Calculate the angles marked with letters.

a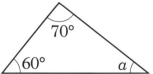

c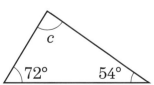

b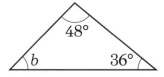

d

Special triangles

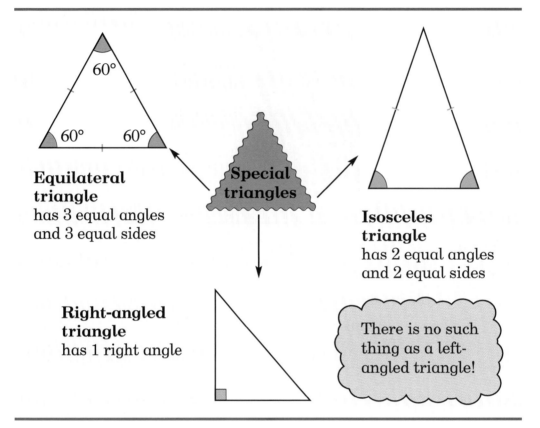

Equilateral triangle has 3 equal angles and 3 equal sides

Special triangles

Isosceles triangle has 2 equal angles and 2 equal sides

Right-angled triangle has 1 right angle

There is no such thing as a left-angled triangle!

Exercise 12:9

1 Copy and complete the table.

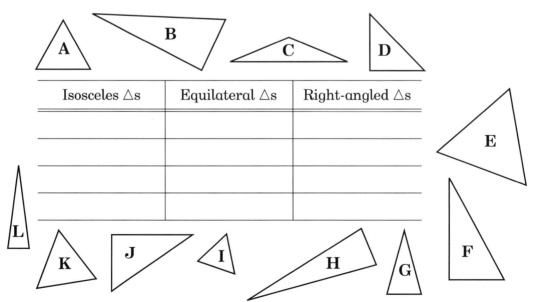

Isosceles △s	Equilateral △s	Right-angled △s

Congruent shapes

Example These three triangles are the same shape.
They have been rotated or reflected but are still the same shape.

They are **congruent** shapes.

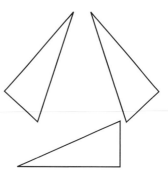

Exercise 12:10

1 These shapes are not congruent to the ones in the example. Can you see why? It may help to trace them.

a 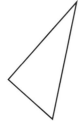   **b**    **c**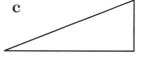

2 For each set of triangles, there is one that is not congruent to the others. Which is the odd one out?

a i   ii   iii   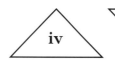 iv   v

b i   ii   iii   iv   v

c i   ii   iii   iv   v

4 Drawing triangles

Mike wants to make an accurate scale drawing of the sail on his sailboard.

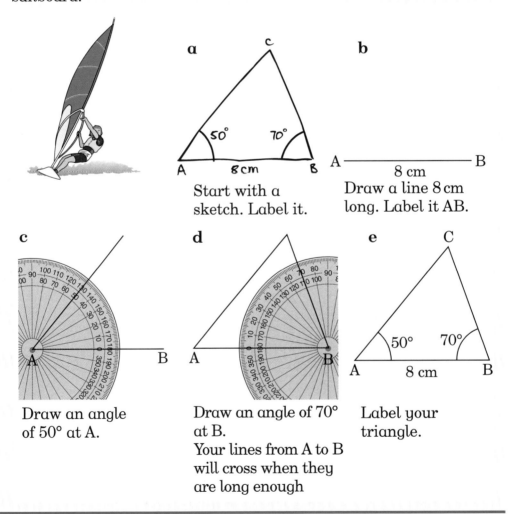

a
50° 70°
A — 8 cm — B
Start with a sketch. Label it.

b
A —— 8 cm —— B
Draw a line 8 cm long. Label it AB.

c
A —— B
Draw an angle of 50° at A.

d
A —— B
Draw an angle of 70° at B.
Your lines from A to B will cross when they are long enough

e
C
50° 70°
A — 8 cm — B
Label your triangle.

Exercise 12:11

1 Make an accurate scale drawing of
the roof of the boat-house.
Start by making a sketch.

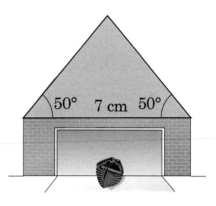

2 Kim has made a model boat to sail on the lake.
There are four different sails from which to choose.

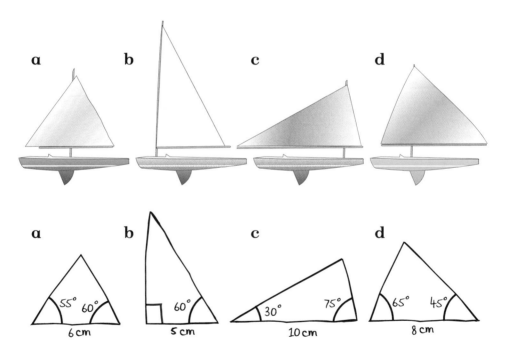

For each model boat:

i copy the sketch

ii make an accurate drawing of the sail.

Which sail would you choose? Give a reason.

1 Copy and complete this table.

Start direction	Turn	New direction	Angle turned
↑ North	Quarter turn anticlockwise	West	
↓ South	Half turn anticlockwise		
→ East	Quarter turn clockwise		
← West	Half turn clockwise		

2 For each angle below:

i say if the angle is acute or obtuse
ii estimate the size of the angle in degrees.

a 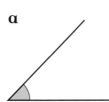 **b**  **c**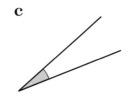

3 Draw these angles.

a 90° **b** 125° **c** 80° **d** 160°

4 Calculate the angles marked with letters.

a 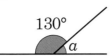 **b** 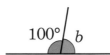 **c**

5 Calculate the angles marked with letters.

a 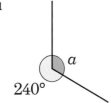 **b** 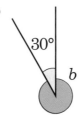 **c**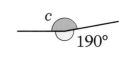

6 Find the angles marked with letters.

a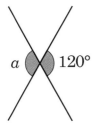

b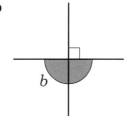

c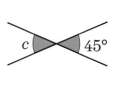

7 Calculate the angles marked with letters.

a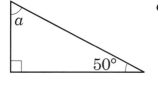

c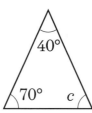

e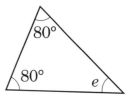

b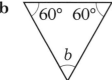

d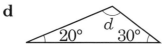

8 For each group of triangles, say which one is **not** congruent to the others.

a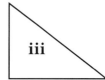

b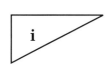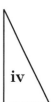

9 Draw these triangles accurately.

a

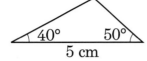

c

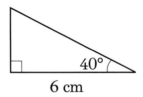

b

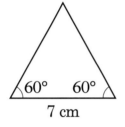

d

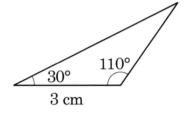

13 Formulas

QUESTIONS

For a moving object

$E = mc^2$

where E = energy,

c is the velocity of light

and m is mass

In simple terms this states that all energy has mass. It was devised by the German-born scientist Albert Einstein.

1 Using letters

Sam works in a cafe.

She takes orders from the customers.

She uses letters to represent each item.

In algebra you can use letters instead of numbers.

Example Sam takes an order for pizza, pizza, pizza and pizza.

She writes $p + p + p + p$

Sam could write this as **4p**

In algebra you can miss out the multiply sign.

So $4 \times p$ is $4p$

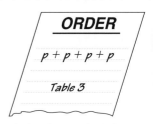

Exercise 13:1

Write each order using algebra.

1 Cola, cola, cola, cola, cola.

2 Lemonade, lemonade, lemonade, lemonade, lemonade, lemonade, lemonade.

3 Pizza, pizza, pizza, pizza, pizza, pizza.

Holly has taken these orders.
Write each one using algebra.
Do not use the multiply sign.

4 $c + c + c + c + c + c + c$

5 $p+p+p+p+p$

6 $l+l+l+l+l+l+l+l+l$

7 $h+h+h+h$

More than one item can be combined in one order.
Write each of these orders using algebra.
Do not use the multiply sign.

8 $c+c+c+l+l+l+l=\,\ldots\ldots\,c+\,\ldots\ldots\,l$

9 $p+p+p+c+c+c+c=\,\ldots\ldots\,p+\,\ldots\ldots\,c$

10 $h+h+p+p+p=$

11 $l+l+c+c+c+p+p+p+p+p=$

12 $h+h+p+c+c+c+c=$

13 $h+h+h+h+h+l+l+l+c+c=$

14 $h+p+h+p+c+l+l+c+l+h=$

Neil is adding up piles of coins.

Each pile has 50p in it.

He has 4 piles of 50p

$50p+50p+50p+50p$
$= 200p$
$= £2.00$

He can write this as a multiplication $4 \times 50p = £2.00$

Multiplication is a quicker way of working out addition.

Exercise 13:2

1 Denise is counting money.
Each pile has 20p in it.

  a Write the sum as an addition.

  b Write the sum as a
    multiplication.

  c Work out how much money Denise has.

2 Michael is counting money.
Each pile has 50p in it.

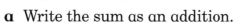
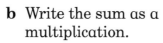
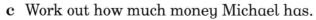

  a Write the sum as an addition.

  b Write the sum as a
    multiplication.

  c Work out how much money Michael has.

3 Barbara is counting money.
Each pile has 10p in it.

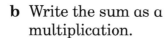

  a Write the sum as an addition.

  b Write the sum as a
    multiplication.

  c Work out how much money Barbara has.

Example   You can write addition sums as multiplications.

$$4 + 4 + 4 + 4 + 4 = 5 \times 4 = 20$$

Write each of these additions as multiplications. Find the answer to
each one.

4 $2 + 2 + 2 + 2 + 2 + 2 = \ldots\ldots \times 2 = \ldots\ldots$

5 $5 + 5 + 5 =$

6 $10 + 10 + 10 + 10 + 10 + 10 + 10 =$

7 $4 + 4 + 4 + 4 =$

 8 $6 + 6 + 6 + 6 + 6 =$

Example

Steven has 3 tubes of sweets $3t$ sweets

He eats 2 sweets -2 sweets

He now has $3t - 2$ sweets

$3t - 2$ is an **expression** for the number of sweets Steven now has.

Write an expression for the number of sweets in each question.

9   Daniel has 3 tubes of sweets.
He eats 4 sweets.

10   Craig has 2 tubes of sweets.
He eats 5 sweets.

11   Lindsey has 5 tubes of sweets.
She eats one sweet.

12   Bob has 3 tubes of sweets.
He eats 2 sweets.

13   Jo has 4 tubes of sweets.
She eats 5 sweets.

Example

Steven has 3 tubes of sweets $3t$ sweets

He friend gives him 2 sweets $+2$ sweets

He now has $3t + 2$ sweets

$3t + 2$ is an **expression** for the number of sweets Steven now has.

Write an expression for the number of sweets in each question.

14 Daniel has 3 tubes of sweets.
His friend gives him 3 sweets.

15 Craig has 2 tubes of sweets.
His friend gives him 3 sweets.

16 Lindsey has 5 tubes of sweets.
Her friend gives her 4 sweets.

17 Bob has 3 tubes of sweets.
His friend gives him 4 sweets.

18 Jo has 4 tubes of sweets.
Her friend gives her 6 sweets.

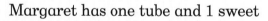

Example Daisy and Margaret each have some sweets.

Daisy has 2 tubes and 3 sweets.

Daisy has $2t + 3$ sweets.

Margaret has one tube and 1 sweet

Margaret has $t + 1$ sweets.

They put their sweets together.

Between them they have
3 tubes and 4 sweets.

They have $3t + 4$ sweets altogether.

This can be written as an algebra sum

$$2t + 3 + t + 1 = 3t + 4$$

In algebra we use t for the number of sweets in a tube because we don't know how many sweets there are in one tube.

Exercise 13:3

1   Paul has these sweets:

Michael has these sweets:

    a Write Paul's sweets using algebra.
    b Write Michael's sweets using algebra.
    c Write an algebra sum for Paul and Michael's sweets added together.

2   Sarah has these sweets:

Louise has these sweets:

    a Write Sarah's sweets using algebra.
    b Write Louise's sweets using algebra.
    c Write an algebra sum for Sarah and Louise's sweets added together.

3   Marie has these sweets:

Jane has these sweets:

    a Write Marie's sweets using algebra.
    b Write Jane's sweets using algebra.
    c Write an algebra sum for Marie and Jane's sweets added together.

4   Ian has these sweets:

Sean has these sweets:

    a Write Ian's sweets using algebra.
    b Write Sean's sweets using algebra.
    c Write an algebra sum for Ian and Sean's sweets added together.

5 Bradley has these sweets:

Nathan has these sweets:

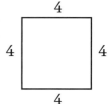

  a Write Bradley's sweets using algebra.
  b Write Nathan's sweets using algebra.
  c Write an algebra sum for Bradley and Nathan's sweets added together.

| **Perimeter** | The total distance around the outside of a shape is its **perimeter**. |

Example   The perimeter of this shape is

$$4 + 4 + 4 + 4 = 4 \times 4$$
$$= 16$$

```
      4
   ┌──────┐
4  │      │  4
   └──────┘
      4
```

Exercise 13:4

1 Find the perimeter of this shape. Use multiplication.

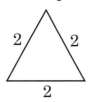

2 Find the perimeter of this shape. Use multiplication.

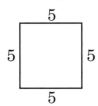

3 Find the perimeter of this shape. Use multiplication.

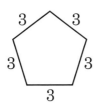

4 Find the perimeter of this shape. Use multiplication.

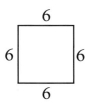

5 Find the perimeter of this shape. Use multiplication.

6 Find the perimeter of this shape. Use multiplication.

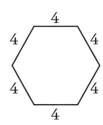

Example   We do not know the length of some of the sides of these polygon shapes.

You can use algebra to write an expression for the perimeter of each polygon shape.

    Perimeter $= s + s + s = 3s$

This polygon has different length sides.

$$\begin{aligned} \text{Perimeter} &= k + k + 3 + 3 + 3 \\ &= 2 \times k + 3 \times 3 \\ &= 2k + 9 \end{aligned}$$

7 Write an expression for the perimeter of this shape.

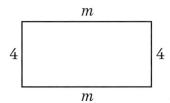

8 Write an expression for the perimeter of this shape.

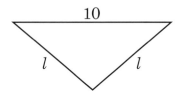

9 Write an expression for the perimeter of this shape.

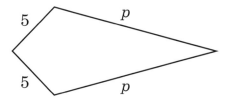

10 Write an expression for the perimeter of this shape.

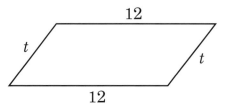

Example   The sides of this polygon are two different lengths. We don't know how long they are.

$$\text{Perimeter} = m + m + m + d + d$$
$$= 3 \times m + 2 \times d$$
$$= 3m + 2d$$

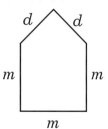

11 Write an expression for the perimeter of this shape.

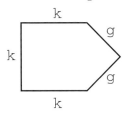

12 Write an expression for the perimeter of this shape.

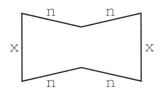

13 Write an expression for the perimeter of this shape.

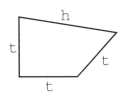

14 Write an expression for the perimeter of this shape.

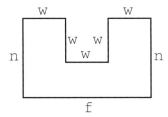

2 Patterns

Mr Love is planning a school trip to the pantomime.

Example One adult is needed to look after two children.

How many children can 2 adults look after?

2 adults can look after 4 children.

Exercise 13:5

1 **a** Draw a picture to show how many children 3 adults can look after.

 b Draw a picture to show how many children 4 adults can look after.

 c Draw a picture to show how many children 5 adults can look after.

 d Copy and complete the table

Adults	1	2	3	4	5
Children	2			8	

 e Copy and complete the sentence.
 'Each time 1 adult is added, ... more children are added.'

Example We can use counters or any other symbol instead of drawing people.

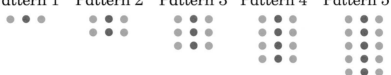

Pattern 1 Pattern 2 Pattern 3 Pattern 4 Pattern 5

Red	1	2	3	4	5
Green	2	4	6	8	10

Each time a new pattern is added 1 more red counter is added.

Each time a new pattern is added 2 more green counters are added.

---

2 On a different school trip 1 adult looks after 3 children.
A driver takes them all on the bus.

2 adults   3 children   3 adults   6 children

We can use counters instead of drawing people.

Pattern 1   Pattern 2

a Draw pictures using counters to show the next three patterns.
b Copy and complete the table.

Adults	2	3	4	5	6
Children	3	6			

c Copy and complete these sentences.
'Each time a new pattern is added … more red counter is added.'
'Each time a new pattern is added … more green counters are added.'

3 Alan is making patterns using red and blue counters.

Pattern 1   Pattern 2   Pattern 3

Alan adds one extra red counter each time.

a Draw Pattern 4 and Pattern 5.

b Fill in the table for all five patterns.

Pattern number	Number of red counters	Number of blue counters	Total number of counters
1	1	1	$1 + 1 = 2$
2	2	1	$2 + 1 = 3$
3	3	1	$3 + 1 =$
4			
5			

c Write down the total number of counters in Pattern 5.

d How many counters will there be all together in Pattern 6?

e Alan's rule for the pattern is $n + 1$.

Pattern number, n ⟶ **+1** ⟶ Total number of counters

    i   Which colour counter does the 1 stand for?
   ii   What does the n stand for?

f In Pattern 10 how many counters will be **i** blue and **ii** red?

3   Function machines

Dilraj uses function machines to solve algebraic equations.

Example $3d + 4 = 10$

Dilraj writes this equation using function machines.

$$d \longrightarrow \boxed{\times 3} \longrightarrow \boxed{+4} \longrightarrow 10$$

He writes the inverse function machine to find the answer.

$$2 \longleftarrow \boxed{\div 3} \longleftarrow \boxed{-4} \longleftarrow 10$$

$d = 2$

Exercise 13:6

2   Solve these equations using inverse function machines.

1 $4p + 2 = 14$

$$p \longrightarrow \boxed{\times 4} \longrightarrow \boxed{+2} \longrightarrow 14$$

$$\ldots\ldots \longleftarrow \boxed{\div \ldots\ldots} \longleftarrow \boxed{- \ldots\ldots} \longleftarrow 14$$

$p = \ldots$

2 $5y + 4 = 9$

$$y \longrightarrow \boxed{\times 5} \longrightarrow \boxed{+4} \longrightarrow 9$$

$$\ldots\ldots \longleftarrow \boxed{\div \ldots\ldots} \longleftarrow \boxed{- \ldots\ldots} \longleftarrow 9$$

$y = \ldots$

3 $6w + 12 = 30$

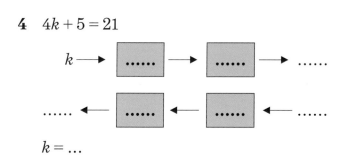

$w = \ldots$

4 $4k + 5 = 21$

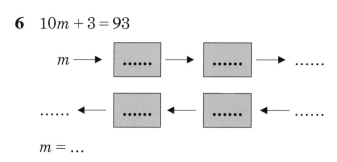

$k = \ldots$

5 $8l + 10 = 90$

$l = \ldots$

6 $10m + 3 = 93$

$m = \ldots$

7 $3t + 12 = 72$

$t = \ldots$

Example $\dfrac{t}{2} + 7 = 21$

Winston writes this equation using function machines

$$t \longrightarrow \boxed{\div 2} \longrightarrow \boxed{+7} \longrightarrow 21$$

He writes the inverse function machine to find the answer.

$$\mathbf{28} \longleftarrow \boxed{\times 2} \longleftarrow \boxed{-7} \longleftarrow 21$$

$t = 28$

H 3   Solve these equations using inverse function machines

8 $\dfrac{f}{5} + 10 = 11$

$$f \longrightarrow \boxed{\div 5} \longrightarrow \boxed{+10} \longrightarrow 11$$

$$\ldots\ldots \longleftarrow \boxed{\times \ldots\ldots} \longleftarrow \boxed{- \ldots\ldots} \longleftarrow 11$$

$f = \ldots$

9 $\dfrac{h}{3} + 8 = 15$

$$h \longrightarrow \boxed{\div \ldots\ldots} \longrightarrow \boxed{+8} \longrightarrow 15$$

$$\ldots\ldots \longleftarrow \boxed{\times \ldots\ldots} \longleftarrow \boxed{- \ldots\ldots} \longleftarrow 15$$

$h = \ldots$

10 $\dfrac{c}{10} + 1 = 5$

$$c \longrightarrow \boxed{\div \ldots\ldots} \longrightarrow \boxed{+ \ldots\ldots} \longrightarrow \ldots\ldots$$

$$\ldots\ldots \longleftarrow \boxed{\times \ldots\ldots} \longleftarrow \boxed{- \ldots\ldots} \longleftarrow 5$$

$c = \ldots$

11 $\dfrac{w}{9} + 3 = 4$

...... $\longrightarrow$ [......] $\longrightarrow$ [......] $\longrightarrow$ ......

...... $\longleftarrow$ [......] $\longleftarrow$ [......] $\longleftarrow$ ......

$w = ...$

12 $\dfrac{t}{8} + 4 = 10$

...... $\longrightarrow$ [......] $\longrightarrow$ [......] $\longrightarrow$ ......

...... $\longleftarrow$ [......] $\longleftarrow$ [......] $\longleftarrow$ ......

$t = ...$

Example $4m - 6 = 10$

Hazel solves this equation using function machines.

$m \longrightarrow$ [×**4**] $\longrightarrow$ [**−6**] $\longrightarrow 10$

She writes the inverse function machine.

4 $\longleftarrow$ [÷**4**] $\longleftarrow$ [**+6**] $\longleftarrow 10$

$m = 4$

H 4 Solve these equations using inverse function machines

13 $4k - 2 = 18$

$k \longrightarrow$ [×**4**] $\longrightarrow$ [**−2**] $\longrightarrow 18$

...... $\longleftarrow$ [÷......] $\longleftarrow$ [+......] $\longleftarrow 18$

$k = ...$

14 $5l - 3 = 17$

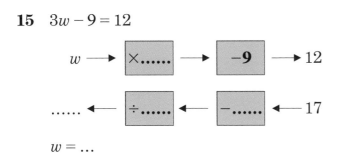

$l = \ldots$

15 $3w - 9 = 12$

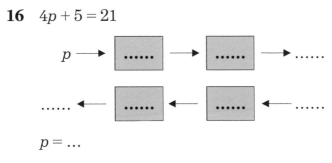

$w = \ldots$

16 $4p + 5 = 21$

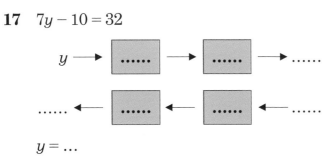

$p = \ldots$

17 $7y - 10 = 32$

$$y \longrightarrow \boxed{\cdots} \longrightarrow \boxed{\cdots} \longrightarrow \ldots$$
$$\ldots \longleftarrow \boxed{\cdots} \longleftarrow \boxed{\cdots} \longleftarrow \ldots$$

$y = \ldots$

18 $10m - 9 = 91$

$$m \longrightarrow \boxed{\cdots} \longrightarrow \boxed{\cdots} \longrightarrow \ldots$$
$$\ldots \longleftarrow \boxed{\cdots} \longleftarrow \boxed{\cdots} \longleftarrow \ldots$$

$m = \ldots$

Example $\dfrac{m}{2} - 5 = 20$

Fiona writes this equation using function machines.

$$m \longrightarrow \boxed{\div 2} \longrightarrow \boxed{-5} \longrightarrow 20$$

She writes the inverse function machine to find the answer.

$$50 \longleftarrow \boxed{\times 2} \longleftarrow \boxed{+5} \longleftarrow 20$$

$m = 50$

H 5 Solve these equations using inverse function machines

19 $\dfrac{f}{2} - 5 = 5$

$$f \longrightarrow \boxed{\div 2} \longrightarrow \boxed{-5} \longrightarrow 5$$

$$\ldots\ldots \longleftarrow \boxed{\times \ldots\ldots} \longleftarrow \boxed{+ \ldots\ldots} \longleftarrow 5$$

$f = \ldots$

20 $\dfrac{h}{3} - 6 = 1$

$$h \longrightarrow \boxed{\div \ldots\ldots} \longrightarrow \boxed{-6} \longrightarrow 1$$

$$\ldots\ldots \longleftarrow \boxed{\times \ldots\ldots} \longleftarrow \boxed{+ \ldots\ldots} \longleftarrow 1$$

$h = \ldots$

21 $\dfrac{d}{10} - 1 = 4$

$$d \longrightarrow \boxed{\div \ldots\ldots} \longrightarrow \boxed{- \ldots\ldots} \longrightarrow \ldots\ldots$$

$$\ldots\ldots \longleftarrow \boxed{\times \ldots\ldots} \longleftarrow \boxed{+ \ldots\ldots} \longleftarrow 4$$

$d = \ldots$

22 $\dfrac{c}{4} - 8 = 12$

$$\ldots\ldots \longrightarrow \boxed{\cdots\cdots} \longrightarrow \boxed{\cdots\cdots} \longrightarrow \ldots\ldots$$

$$\ldots\ldots \longleftarrow \boxed{\cdots\cdots} \longleftarrow \boxed{\cdots\cdots} \longleftarrow \ldots\ldots$$

$c = \ldots$

23 $\dfrac{d}{3} - 13 = 2$

$$\ldots\ldots \longrightarrow \boxed{\cdots\cdots} \longrightarrow \boxed{\cdots\cdots} \longrightarrow \ldots\ldots$$

$$\ldots\ldots \longleftarrow \boxed{\cdots\cdots} \longleftarrow \boxed{\cdots\cdots} \longleftarrow \ldots\ldots$$

$d = \ldots$

24 $\dfrac{t}{5} - 6 = 10$

$$\ldots\ldots \longrightarrow \boxed{\cdots\cdots} \longrightarrow \boxed{\cdots\cdots} \longrightarrow \ldots\ldots$$

$$\ldots\ldots \longleftarrow \boxed{\cdots\cdots} \longleftarrow \boxed{\cdots\cdots} \longleftarrow \ldots\ldots$$

$t = \ldots$

Exercise 13:7

Solve these equations. Use inverse function machines to help you.

1 $3w + 10 = 16$

2 $\dfrac{t}{2} - 6 = 6$

3 $\dfrac{m}{5} + 10 = 11$

4 $5x + 4 = 19$

5 $\dfrac{t}{5} - 6 = 10$

6 $7f - 7 = 21$

7 $\dfrac{h}{10} + 2 = 32$

8 $9x - 5 = 40$

Investigating missing numbers – Arithmagons

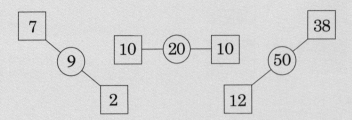

Can you work out how to make the numbers in the circles from the numbers in the squares?

1 Write down the rule for finding the numbers in the circles.

2 Find the numbers in the circles in these puzzles.

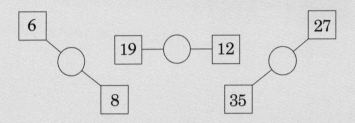

Can you work out how to find the missing number in these puzzles?

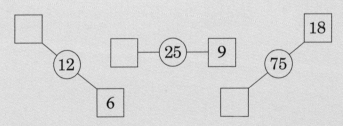

3 Write down the rule for finding the missing numbers in these puzzles.

4 Find the missing numbers in these puzzles.

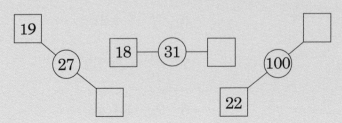

These puzzles have letters as well as numbers.
You use the same rules for finding the missing numbers.
Can you work out what *a* and *b* must be in these puzzles?

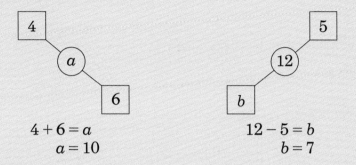

$$4 + 6 = a$$
$$a = 10$$

$$12 - 5 = b$$
$$b = 7$$

5   Work out the value of the letters in these puzzles.

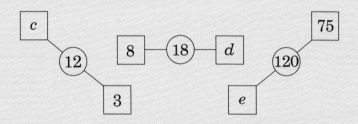

6   Make up 8 number puzzles like these and give them to a friend to work out.

These puzzles have more than 2 squares.

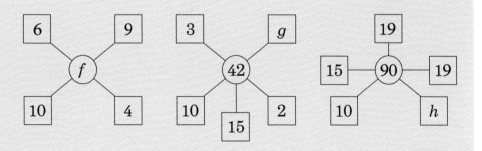

7   Find the value of the letters in these puzzles.

8   Make up 5 number puzzles like these and give them to a friend to work out.

You can change the rule for finding the number in the circle.

Can you work out the rule for these puzzles?
They all have the same rule.

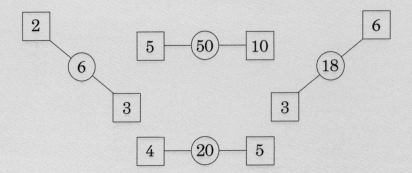

9 Write down the rule for finding the numbers in the circles.

10 Make up some puzzles of your own.
Write down the rule for each one.

1 Sheila takes these orders in a café. Write each order using algebra.
 a Lemonade, lemonade, lemonade.
 b Pizza, pizza, pizza, pizza, pizza.

2 Write these in a more simple way.
 a $p + p + p + p + h + h$ **b** $l + l + l + m + m + m + m$

3 Frankie is counting money.
 Each pile has 50p in it.

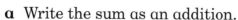

 a Write the sum as an addition.
 b Write the sum as a
 multiplication.
 c Work out how much money Frankie has.

4 Write these additions as multiplications and find the total.
 a $3 + 3 + 3 + 3 = \ldots\ldots \times 3 = \ldots\ldots$ **b** $7 + 7 + 7 + 7 + 7 + 7 =$

5 Carla has 2 tubes of sweets.
 She eats 2 sweets.
 Write an expression for the
 number of sweets Carla now has.

6 Claire has 1 tube of sweets.
 Her sister gives her 3 sweets.
 Write an expression for the number
 of sweets Claire now has.

7 Michelle has 2 tubes and 2 sweets. David has 3 tubes and 1 sweet.
 a Write an expression for the number of sweets Michelle has.
 b Write an expression for the number of sweets David has.
 c Write an algebra sum for Michelle and David's sweets added
 together.

8 Find the perimeter of this shape. Use multiplication.

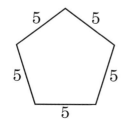

9 Write an expression for the perimeter of this shape.

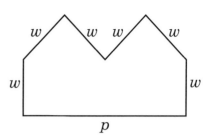

10 On a school trip one adult looks after 4 children.

a Draw pictures using people to show the next three patterns.

b Copy and complete the table.

Adults	1	2	3	4
Children	4			

c Copy and complete this sentence.
'Each time there is an extra adult there are ⋯⋯ more children. The number of children goes up in ⋯⋯.'

11 Peter is making patterns from counters

Pattern 1   Pattern 2   Pattern 3

● ● ●   ● ● ● ●   ● ● ● ● ●

a Draw the next two patterns.

b How many counters will there be altogether in Pattern 6?

c Copy and complete this table.

	Pattern 1	Pattern 2	Pattern 3	Pattern 4	Pattern 5
Blue counters		2			
Red counters		2			
Total		4			

Peter's rule for the pattern is $c + 2$

d Which colour counter does the 2 stand for?

e Which colour counter does the c stand for?

12 Solve these equations using inverse function machines.

a $2k + 4 = 10$ **b** $\dfrac{m}{3} - 2 = 10$

14 Fractions

QUESTIONS

Fold a sheet of paper in half, and in half again, and again as many times as you can.

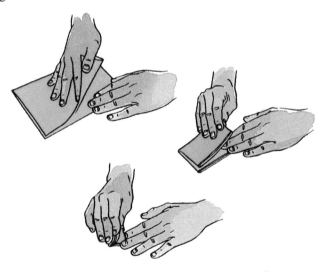

How many times can you fold the paper?

You will not be able to fold it more than six times.

1 Fractions

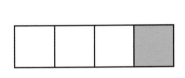
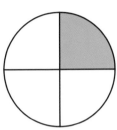

In each picture, $\frac{1}{4}$ is coloured blue.

1 part is coloured blue.

There are 4 parts altogether.

One quarter is coloured blue.

$\frac{1}{4}$ is coloured blue.

Exercise 14:1

You need some sheets of plain paper for this exercise.

1 a Fold a sheet of paper in **half**.
    Unfold your paper.
  b How many parts is your paper divided into?
  c How many halves make a whole?

2 a Fold a sheet of paper in half.
    Fold it in half again.
    Unfold your paper.
  b How many parts is your paper divided into?
  c How many quarters make a whole?
  d Write one quarter using figures.

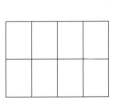

3 This time fold the paper in half three times.
  Unfold it. It should look like this:
  a How many parts is your paper divided into?
  b How many eighths make a whole?
  c Write one eighth using figures.

Example   Look at the diagram.   *Answers*

a How many parts are blue?   3

b How many parts is the diagram   4
   divided into?

c What fraction is blue? $\frac{3}{4}$

d How many parts are red?   1

e What fraction is red? $\frac{1}{4}$

4 Look at the diagram.

   a How many parts are blue?

   b How many parts is the diagram
      divided into?

   c What fraction is blue?

   d How many parts are red?

   e What fraction is red?

5 Look at the diagram.

   a How many parts are blue?

   b How many parts is the diagram divided into?

   c What fraction is blue?

   d How many parts are red?

   e What fraction is red?

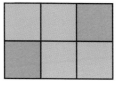

W 1   6 Fractions can be described in diagrams, words and figures.
          Copy the table. Complete the missing sections in the table.
          The first one has been done for you.

	Diagrams	Words	Figures
a		Two thirds	$\frac{2}{3}$
b	Shade	...	$\frac{3}{4}$
c		...	...
d	Shade	Five eighths	...

Dividing whole numbers into fractions

Example Eleanor has two cakes.

She divides each cake into quarters.

There are 4 pieces in one cake.

Altogether there are 8 pieces in two cakes.

There are 8 quarters in two cakes.

Exercise 14:2

1 **a** How many halves are there in one cake?

   b How many halves make two cakes?

   c How many halves make three cakes?

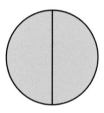

2 **a** How many eighths are there in one cake?

   b How many eighths are there in two cakes?

   c How many eighths are there in three cakes?

3 At a party there are three cakes.
Each cake us cut into tenths.
How many pieces are there altogether?

4 Mike has two bars of chocolate.
Each bar is divided into sixths.
How many pieces does he have altogether?

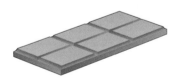

5 Imran has four bars of chocolate.
Each bar is divided into eighths.
How many pieces does he have altogether?

$\frac{5}{4}$ is the same as five quarters.

The top number is larger than the bottom number.
The fraction is 'top heavy'.

Look at the diagram.
Five quarters make one whole and one quarter.

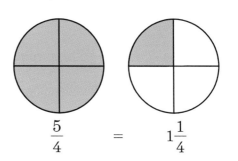

$\frac{5}{4}$ $=$ $1\frac{1}{4}$

Exercise 14:3

 2   Write each of these as:

a a 'top heavy fraction',

b a whole number and a fraction.

1   **2**

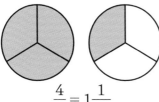

$\frac{4}{3} = 1\frac{1}{...}$

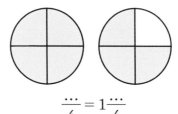

$\frac{...}{4} = 1\frac{...}{4}$

3

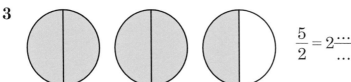

$\frac{5}{2} = 2\frac{...}{...}$

4

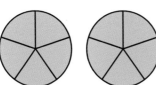

$\frac{12}{5} = ...\ ...$

5

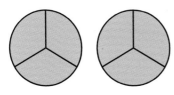

$... = ...$

Example   Christie has to find $\frac{1}{5}$ of 20.

She uses counters to help her.

She shares the counters out into 5 equal piles.

There are **4** counters in each pile.

$\frac{1}{5}$ of 20 is **4**.

Exercise 14:4

You can use counters or blocks to help you with this exercise.

1 Jason has to find $\frac{1}{4}$ of 12.

   a Divide 12 counters into 4 equal piles.

   b How many counters are there in each pile?

   c Copy this sum and fill in the answer.

     $\frac{1}{4}$ of 12 = ...

2 Rob has to find $\frac{1}{5}$ of 15.

   a Divide 15 counters into 5 equal piles.

   b How many counters are there in each pile?

   c Copy this sum and fill in the answer.

     $\frac{1}{5}$ of 15 = ...

3 Use counters to find the answers to these sums.

   a $\frac{1}{4}$ of 12   **d** $\frac{1}{3}$ of 30   **g** $\frac{1}{2}$ of 10

   b $\frac{1}{3}$ of 9   **e** $\frac{1}{2}$ of 14   **h** $\frac{1}{4}$ of 20

   c $\frac{1}{5}$ of 25   **f** $\frac{1}{4}$ of 16   **i** $\frac{1}{3}$ of 15

Example Phil has no counters.

He needs to find $\frac{1}{5}$ of 10.

Phil knows he needs to divide 10 into five groups.

To find $\frac{1}{5}$ you divide by 5:

$10 \div 5 = 2$ $\frac{1}{5}$ of 10 is 2.

W 3 *Exercise 14:5*

1 a Write down the number you divide by to find a $\frac{1}{2}$.

b Complete the table. The first one has been done for you.

Find		Answer
$\frac{1}{2}$ of 8	$8 \div 2$	4
$\frac{1}{2}$ of 10		
$\frac{1}{2}$ of 6		

2 a Write down the number you divide by to find $\frac{1}{3}$.

b Complete the table.

Find		Answer
$\frac{1}{3}$ of 6		
$\frac{1}{3}$ of 9		
$\frac{1}{3}$ of 12		

3 a Write down the number you divide by to find $\frac{1}{4}$.

b Complete the table.

Find		Answer
$\frac{1}{4}$ of 8		
$\frac{1}{4}$ of 20		
$\frac{1}{4}$ of 16		

4 a Write down the number you divide by to find $\frac{1}{8}$.

b Complete the table.

Find		Answer
$\frac{1}{8}$ of 8		
$\frac{1}{8}$ of 16		
$\frac{1}{8}$ of 32		

James has a bar of chocolate.
It is divided into 16 pieces.

He wants to keep $\frac{3}{4}$ of the chocolate
and give away the rest to his
friends.

How many pieces will he keep?

James first needs to calculate the number of pieces in $\frac{1}{4}$ of the bar.

James divides 16 by 4.

$$\frac{1}{4} \text{ of } 16 = 4$$

$$\text{so } \frac{3}{4} \text{ of } 16 = 3 \times 4$$

$$= 12$$

James keeps 12 pieces of chocolate.

5 **a** What is $\frac{1}{5}$ of 20?

    b What is $\frac{3}{5}$ of 20?

6 **a** What is $\frac{1}{3}$ of 12?

    b What is $\frac{2}{3}$ of 12?

7 **a** What is $\frac{1}{4}$ of 8?

    b What is $\frac{3}{4}$ of 8?

8 **a** What is $\frac{1}{6}$ of 24?

    b What is $\frac{3}{6}$ of 24?

 1,2

9 What is $\frac{2}{3}$ of 9?

10 What is $\frac{3}{8}$ of 16?

How do you divide **seven** cakes between **four** children?

Each wants an equal share.

You have to work out $7 \div 4$.

The children each get **one whole** cake.

The remaining **three** cakes are cut into **four** quarters.

$7 \div 4$ can be written as $\dfrac{7}{4} = 1\dfrac{3}{4}$

Each child gets $1\dfrac{3}{4}$ cakes.

Exercise 14:6

1 Share three apples equally between the two children.

Copy and complete.

$3 \div 2 = \dfrac{3}{2} = \ldots$

Each child gets ... apples.

2 Share five chocolate bars between three children.

   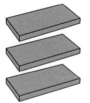

Copy and complete.

$5 \div 3 = \dots = \dots$

Each child gets … chocolate bars.

3 Share five cakes between four children.

Copy and complete.

$5 \div 4 = \dots = \dots$

Each child gets … cakes.

4 Share two oranges between three children.

Copy and complete.

$2 \div 3 = \dots$

Each child gets … of an orange.

2   Equivalent fractions

· ·

Example   Jane folds a piece of paper into quarters.
She colours half of the paper red.

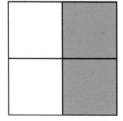

  a How many squares are red?

  b How many squares are there
altogether?

  c What fraction of the square is red?
Write the fraction in more than one way.

  a 2 squares are red.

  b There are 4 squares
altogether.

  c $\dfrac{2}{4}$ of the square is red.

 is the same as

$\dfrac{2}{4}$ $\dfrac{1}{2}$

Exercise 14:7

  1 Jane folds another piece of paper into sixths.
She colours half of the paper blue.

    a How many squares are blue?

    b How many squares are there altogether?

    c What fraction of the rectangle is blue?
Write the fraction in more than one way.

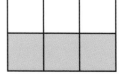

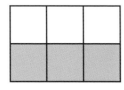   is the same as 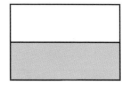

    ...   =   ...

  2 Jane folds another piece of paper into eighths.
She colours half of the paper blue.

    a How many squares are blue?

    b How many squares are there altogether?

    c What fraction of the rectangle is blue?
Write the fraction in more than one way.

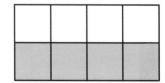

3 Which of these diagrams show a half?

a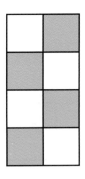

d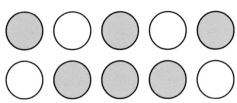

b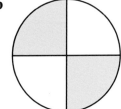

e

c

f

W 5 **4** **Take half**   Using the grids provided colour half of each grid.
For example,

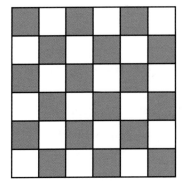

W 6

Below are two bars of chocolate. They are the same size, but are divided into pieces in different ways.

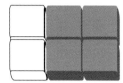   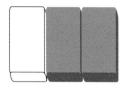

Number of white pieces = 2   Number of white pieces = 1

Total number of pieces = 6   Total number of pieces = 3

Fraction white = $\dfrac{2}{6}$ Fraction white = $\dfrac{1}{3}$

The same amount of each bar of chocolate is white,

$$\text{so} \quad \frac{2}{6} = \frac{1}{3}$$

5 In each part the bars of chocolate are the same size.

a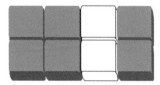

Complete the following:

Number of white pieces = ...   Number of white pieces = ...
Total number of pieces = ...   Total number of pieces = ...
Fraction white = ...   Fraction white = ...

So ... = ...

b

Complete the following:

Number of white pieces = ...   Number of white pieces = ...
Total number of pieces = ...   Total number of pieces = ...
Fraction white = ...   Fraction white = ...

So ... = ...

c

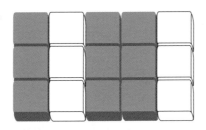

Complete the following:

Number of white pieces = ...   Number of white pieces = ...

Total number of pieces = ...   Total number of pieces = ...

Fraction white = ...   Fraction white = ...

So ... = ...

H 1   **6** Shade the diagrams to show that the fractions are equal.

a $\dfrac{1}{5} = \dfrac{2}{10}$

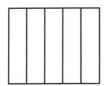   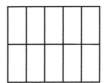

b $\dfrac{2}{3} = \dfrac{4}{6}$

   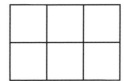

Draw your own diagrams to show:

c $\dfrac{3}{4} = \dfrac{6}{8}$

d $\dfrac{1}{2} = \dfrac{3}{6}$

e $\dfrac{1}{3} = \dfrac{3}{9}$

3   Using a calculator

Liam and Noel want to change $\frac{3}{5}$ to a decimal.

Noel has found the answer using his calculator.

Noel divides the top number by the bottom number to convert a fraction to a decimal.

Example $\frac{3}{5}$ **3** **÷** **5** **=** $\boxed{0.6}$

top ÷ bottom =

Answer $\frac{3}{5} = 0.6$

This works for any fraction.

Exercise 14:8

1   Complete this table.

Fraction	Keys to press	Decimal
$\frac{1}{4}$	**1** **÷** **4** **=**	
$\frac{1}{2}$		
$\frac{3}{4}$		
$\frac{1}{10}$		

You should now learn the fractions and decimals in the table.

2   Change these fractions into decimals using a calculator.

a $\frac{4}{5}$ b $\frac{6}{8}$ c $\frac{9}{12}$ d $\frac{12}{20}$ e $\frac{3}{10}$ f $\frac{3}{50}$

2

3 By first changing each fraction to a decimal, link the fractions that are equal. One equal pair has been found already.

$$\frac{4}{10} = \dots \qquad \frac{1}{2} = 0.5$$

$$\frac{6}{8} = \dots \qquad \frac{2}{5} = \dots$$

$$\frac{3}{6} = 0.5 \qquad \frac{3}{4} = \dots$$

4 Which fractions from this list are equal to $\frac{1}{2}$?

You may want to change some of the fractions into decimals to help you.

$$\left(\frac{1}{2} \text{ as a decimal is } 0.5 \right) \qquad \frac{50}{100} \quad \frac{3}{4} \quad \frac{4}{8} \quad \frac{3}{5} \quad \frac{16}{32}$$

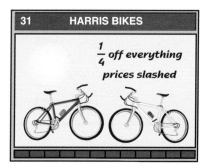

Mountain bike	£160	Cycling jersey	£18
Helmet	£40	Cycling gloves	£5
Shorts	£12	Cycling Bottle	£2

Example Ben wants to buy the shorts and the cycle bottle.

a How much will Ben save on:

Shorts

$\frac{1}{4}$ of $12 = 12 \div 4$
      $= £3$

Cycling bottle

$\frac{1}{4}$ of £2 = £0.50

b What does Ben pay for:

Shorts

£12 − £3 = £9

Cycling bottle

£2 − £0.50 = £1.50

As we are using money we must always have 2 figures after the decimal point, even if the last figure is zero.

Exercise 14:9

 3 If there is a $\frac{1}{4}$ off each of these items work out:

1 For each of the items work out
   i how much you save
   ii the new price.

a

£160

c

£18

b

£40

d
£6

 4 **2**

Dog basket	£18
Cat basket	£12
Dog food	£9

KEY PETS 127

$\frac{1}{3}$ off everything

For each of the items work out
   i how much you save
   ii the new price.

 4 **a**

£18

b

£12

c
£9

COMPLETE DOG FOOD

3 Find **a** $\frac{1}{8}$ of £20 **b** $\frac{1}{10}$ of £4 **c** $\frac{1}{4}$ of £9

1 Look at the diagram.

a How many parts are blue?
b How many parts is the diagram divided into?
c What fraction is blue?

d How many parts are red?
e What fraction is red?

2 Look at each of the diagrams.
Write down the fraction that is blue and the fraction that is red.

a

Fraction blue = ...
Fraction red = ...

b

Fraction blue = ...
Fraction red = ...

c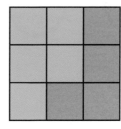

Fraction blue = ...
Fraction red = ...

H 5   3 How many halves are there in four cakes?

H 5   4 How many quarters are there in three cakes?

H 5   5 Meg has three bars of chocolate.
Each bar is divided into sixths.
How many pieces does she have altogether?

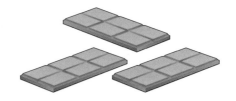

6 Write each of these:

i as a top heavy fraction   ii as a whole number and a fraction.

$$\frac{...}{4} = ...$$

$$\frac{...}{6} = ...$$

7 Write down the number you divide by to find:

a $\dfrac{1}{3}$ **b** $\dfrac{1}{5}$ **c** $\dfrac{1}{4}$ **d** $\dfrac{1}{10}$

W 9

8 Complete the table. The first line has been done for you.

Find	Answer	
$\frac{1}{4}$ of 8	$8 \div 4$	2
$\frac{1}{5}$ of 25	$25 \div \ldots$	$\ldots$
$\frac{1}{3}$ of 9	$9 \div \ldots$	$\ldots$
$\frac{1}{4}$ of 16	$\ldots \div \ldots$	$\ldots$
$\frac{1}{10}$ of 60	$\ldots \div \ldots$	$\ldots$

9 a What is $\dfrac{1}{5}$ of 20? **b** What is $\dfrac{2}{5}$ of 20?

10 a What is $\dfrac{1}{3}$ of 18? **b** What is $\dfrac{2}{3}$ of 18?

11 a What is $\dfrac{1}{10}$ of 40? **b** What is $\dfrac{9}{10}$ of 40?

12 Share 4 cakes between 3 children. Write the answer as a fraction.

13 Which of these fractions are equal to $\dfrac{1}{2}$?

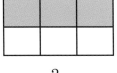 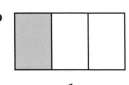 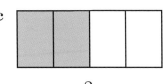

a $\dfrac{3}{6}$ **b** $\dfrac{1}{3}$ **c** $\dfrac{2}{4}$

6 **14** Shade diagrams to show that these fractions are equal.

a $\dfrac{1}{2} = \dfrac{4}{8}$ **b** $\dfrac{1}{3} = \dfrac{2}{6}$ **c** $\dfrac{5}{10} = \dfrac{1}{2}$

7 **15** Link with an arrow the fractions and decimals that are equal. The first one is done for you.

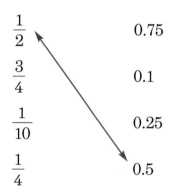

$\dfrac{1}{2}$ 0.75

$\dfrac{3}{4}$ 0.1

$\dfrac{1}{10}$ 0.25

$\dfrac{1}{4}$ 0.5

16 Change these fractions into decimals using a calculator.

a $\dfrac{3}{5}$ **b** $\dfrac{7}{10}$ **c** $\dfrac{8}{20}$ **d** $\dfrac{4}{8}$

17

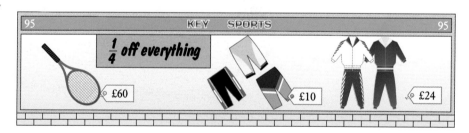

For each of the items below work out:

i how much you save

ii the new price.

a tennis racket   **b** track suit   **c** cycling shorts

15 The best chapter, probably

QUESTIONS

A hurricane is an intense, devastating tropical storm caused by a low-pressure weather system. Hurricanes occur in tropical regions usually between July and October.

Weather forecasters try to warn people of the approach of a hurricane. The forecasters use probabilities to give an idea of the likelihood of a hurricane striking a particular area.

1   Counters and spinners

There are 10 counters in a bag.

Some are red. The rest are black.

Without looking David and Pavneet take it in turns to take a counter.

They write down the colour.

They always put the counter back.

They do this lots of times.

They are trying to find out how many counters of each colour are in the bag without looking.

Exercise 15:1

Your teacher will give you a bag with 10 counters, of two different colours, in it.

 1

You need a tally-table worksheet.

1 a Take a counter out of the bag without looking.

Colour	Tally	Frequency
	ЖНТ I	

b Put a tally on tally-table 1.

c Put the counter back.

d Take a counter 10 times. Mark a tally each time.

e Write the total for each colour in the frequency column.

2 a Take a counter out of the bag without looking.

b Put a tally on tally-table 2.

c Put the counter back.

d Take a counter 10 times. Mark a tally each time.

e Write the total for each colour in the frequency column.

3 **a** Take a counter out of the bag without looking.

b Put a tally on tally-table 3.

c Put the counter back.

d Take a counter 10 times. Mark a tally each time.

e Write the total for each colour in the frequency column.

Colour	Tally	Frequency
Red	ЖНТ I	6
Green	IIII	4

4 **a** Look at your results.
Are the totals the same for all of your tally-tables 1, 2 and 3?

b Write down how many counters of each colour you think there are in the bag.

c Look in the bag. Write down how many counters there are of each colour.

d How close was your answer?

5 Your teacher will give you another bag with different counters in it.
Carry out this experiment again.
Try and find out the number of counters of each colour without looking.

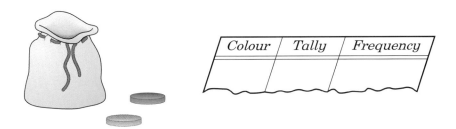

Colour	Tally	Frequency

You can take out counters more than three times to help you work out the number of counters in the bag.

Exercise 15:2

1   Sarah puts these counters in a bag.

Sarah takes a counter without looking.

   a Which colour counter is Sarah most likely to pick?

   b Which colour counter is Sarah least likely to pick?

2   Selina puts these counters in a bag.

Selina takes a counter without looking.

   a Which colour counter is Selina most likely to pick?

   b Which colour counter is Selina least likely to pick?

3   Daniel puts these counters in a bag.

Daniel takes a counter without looking.

   a Which colour counter is Daniel most likely to pick?

   b Which colour counter is Daniel least likely to pick?

4   Jack puts these counters in a bag.

Jack takes a counter without looking.

   a Which colour counter is Jack most likely to pick?

   b Which colour counter is Jack least likely to pick?

Example   If the number of counters of each colour is the same, each colour has an equally likely chance of being chosen.

Red is more likely to be picked because there are more red counters.

Lili adds 2 blue counters to the bag.

Red and blue have an **equally likely chance** of being picked because there are the same number of red and blue counters.

5   Jodi has these counters in a bag.

   a   Which colour counter is Jodi most likely to pick?
   b   Which colour counter is Jodi least likely to pick?
   c   Jodi wants each colour to have an equally likely chance of being picked. What extra counters does Jodi have to add to her bag?

6   Sonya has these counters in a bag.

   a   Which colour counter is Sonya most likely to pick?
   b   Which colour counter is Sonya least likely to pick?
   c   Sonya wants each colour to have an equally likely chance of being picked. What extra counters does Sonya have to add to her bag?

7   Tim has these counters in a bag.

   a   Which colour counter is Tim most likely to pick?
   b   Which colour counter is Tim least likely to pick?
   c   Tim wants each colour to have an equally likely chance of being picked. What extra counters does Tim have to add to his bag?

8 Leslie has these counters in a bag.

   a Which colour counter is Leslie most likely to pick?

   b Which colour counter is Leslie least likely to pick?

   c Leslie wants each colour to have an equally likely chance of being picked. What extra counters does Leslie have to add to her bag?

Danny knows that his bag contains these 10 counters. He doesn't know how many of each colour there are.

Danny picks a counter from the bag without looking.

He writes down the colour and puts it back in the bag.

Danny does this 10 times.

He *expects* to get 7 red counters and 3 yellow counters.

Danny picks a counter from the bag 50 times without looking.
For 10 turns, he expects to get 7 red and 3 yellow counters.
For 50 turns

$$10 \longrightarrow \boxed{\times 5} \longrightarrow 50$$

he would expect to get

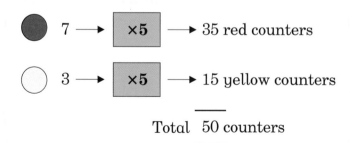

     $7 \longrightarrow \boxed{\times 5} \longrightarrow 35$ red counters

     $3 \longrightarrow \boxed{\times 5} \longrightarrow 15$ yellow counters

            Total 50 counters

Exercise 15:3

1 Danny picks a counter from the same bag **20** times.
   a How many yellows does he expect to get?
   b How many reds does he expect to get?

2 Danny picks a counter from the same bag **30** times.
   a How many yellows does he expect to get?
   b How many reds does he expect to get?

3 Danny picks a counter from the same bag **40** times.
   a How many yellows does he expect to get?
   b How many reds does he expect to get?

4 Danny picks a counter from the same bag **50** times.
   a How many yellows does he expect to get?
   b How many reds does he expect to get?

If you roll a six-sided dice 6 times you would expect to get one of each number.

If you roll a six-sided dice 12 times you would expect to get two of each number.

Helen is trying to get

She rolls the dice **6** times.

She expects to get one

---

5 Sean rolls the dice **6** times.
How many fours would you expect him to get?

6 Ian rolls the dice **12** times.
How many fours would you expect him to get?

7 Philip rolls the dice **18** times.
How many fours would you expect him to get?

8 Marie rolls the dice **24** times.
How many fours would you expect her to get?

This spinner has 4 equal sections.

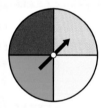

If you spin the spinner four times you would expect to get one of each colour.

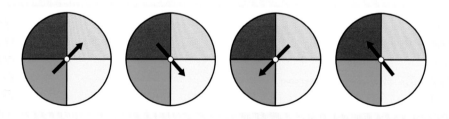

If you spin the spinner eight times you would expect to get two of each colour.

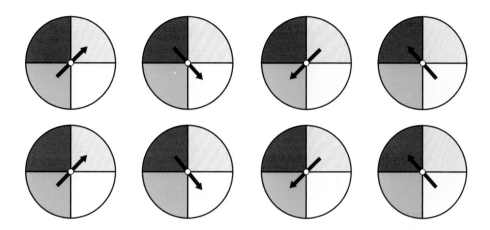

Viv is trying to get red on the spinner.
She spins it 4 times.
She expects to get one red.

---

9 Steven spins the spinner **4** times.
How many greens would you expect him to get?

10 Sarah-Jane spins the spinner **8** times.
How many greens would you expect her to get?

11 Bradley spins the spinner **12** times.
How many greens would you expect him to get?

12 Louise spins the spinner **40** times.
How many greens would you expect her to get?

13 Lindsey spins the spinner **100** times.
How many greens would you expect her to get?

2   How much chance?

Paul and Liz are playing 'Flounders'.

Paul needs a to win.

Paul needs 1 number.

There are 6 numbers on the dice.

Each number has an **equally likely chance** of being rolled.

The probability of getting is $\frac{1}{6}$.

Example   Fiona is using a four-sided dice.
She needs to roll a three.

Fiona needs **1** number.
There are **4** numbers on the dice.

Each number has an **equally likely chance** of being rolled.

The probability of rolling a three is $\frac{1}{4}$.

Exercise 15:4

1   Mark rolls a four-sided dice. Write down the probability that he gets:

   a
      four

   b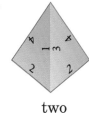
      two

   c
      one

2 Liz rolls a six-sided dice. Write down the probability that she gets:

a   b   c   d

Example

Sally has 3 tins of soup. The labels have come off.
She knows she bought 1 tin of chicken soup and 2 tins of vegetable soup.

There is **1** tin of chicken soup. There are **3** tins altogether.
Each tin has an **equal chance** of being chosen.

The probability that she opens a tin of chicken soup is $\frac{1}{3}$.

---

3 Manuel has 5 tins of soup, but the labels have come off.

He bought 3 tins of tomato and 2 tins of chicken soup.
Manuel opens a tin. Each tin has an **equal chance** of being chosen.

a Write down the probability that the tin contains tomato soup.

b Write down the probability that the tin contains chicken soup.

4   Angela has 6 tins of soup, but the labels have come off.

She bought 1 tin of tomato, 2 tins of chicken and 3 tins of vegetable soup.
Angela opens a tin. Each tin has an **equal chance** of being chosen.

a Write down the probability that the tin contains tomato soup.

b Write down the probability that the tin contains chicken soup.

Example   David has 10 counters in a bag. There are 6 red and 4 green. He finds the probability that he chooses a red counter without looking. Each counter has an **equal chance** of being chosen.

There are **6** red counters. There are **10** counters altogether.

The probability that David chooses a red counter is $\dfrac{6}{10}$.

---

5   Rachel has a bag with **8** counters. There are **5** blue and **3** yellow. Rachel chooses a counter without looking. Each counter has an **equal chance** of being chosen.

a Write down the probability that Rachel chooses yellow.

b Write down the probability that Rachel chooses blue.

6   Bethan has a bag with **7** counters. There are **5** pink and **2** yellow. Bethan chooses a counter without looking. Each counter has an **equal chance** of being chosen.

a Write down the probability that Bethan chooses yellow.

b Write down the probability that Bethan chooses pink.

7   Stefan has a bag with 12 counters. There are 5 green, 4 red and 3 orange.
Stefan chooses a counter without looking. Each counter has an **equal chance** of being chosen.

a Write down the probability that Stefan chooses green.

b Write down the probability that Stefan chooses red.

c Write down the probability that Stefan chooses orange.

This is a six-sided dice with different numbers. Each number is not equally likely to be rolled.

There are 2 ones. The probability of rolling one is $\frac{2}{6}$.

There are 2 twos. The probability of rolling two is $\frac{2}{6}$.

There is 1 three. The probability of rolling three is $\frac{1}{6}$.

There is 1 four. The probability of rolling four is $\frac{1}{6}$.

There are no fives. The probability of rolling five is $\frac{0}{6} = 0$

There are no sixes. The probability of rolling six is $\frac{0}{0} = 0$

8 Jason has a dice with these numbers.

    a Write down the probability Jason rolls a one.
    b Write down the probability Jason rolls a two.
    c Write down the probability Jason rolls a three.
    d Write down the probability Jason rolls a four.

H 1, 2   **9** Christie has a dice with these numbers.

    a Write down the probability that Christie rolls a six.
    b Write down the probability that Christie rolls a two.
    c Write down the probability that Christie rolls a three.
    d Write down the probability that Christie rolls a one.
    e Write down the probability that Christie rolls a five.

Example   Delia likes chocolate. She does not like onions.

Delia has 50 p to spend. She can choose from chocolate and onions. Chocolate and onions **do not have an equal chance** of being chosen by Delia!

Exercise 15:5

For each question write down true or false.

1   There is an equal chance of Kayleigh choosing milk or cola from the school canteen.

2   Heads and tails do not have an equal chance of being thrown on a 2 p coin.

3   Each colour of this spinner has an equal chance of being spun.

4   Katie can choose from cross-country running and rounders in PE. Both sports have an equal chance of being chosen.

3 Probability methods and scales

Jane and Rob are going camping in July. They want to know if it will rain on their trip.
They look at *data* for the weather in July in past years.

They can **estimate the probability** that it will rain on their trip.

There are **three** methods for estimating probability.

Method 1

Look at past data

Method 2

Do a survey or experiment

Method 3

Equally likely outcomes

Date	Rainfall
July 1998	
July 1999	
July 2000	

	Tally	Frequency
Dog	‖‖ ‖‖ ‖	
Cat	‖‖ ‖‖ ‖	
Rabbit	‖	

Example   Niall wants to estimate the probability that someone prefers rock music to dance music. He has to choose a method to use.
There is *no* past data.
There are *no* equally likely outcomes.

Niall does a survey in his school. He uses the results to estimate the probability that someone prefers rock music to dance music.

Exercise 15:6

For each question write down which method you would use to estimate the probability. Write **data**, **survey/experiment**, or **equally likely outcomes**.

1 The probability that it will rain on school sports day.

2 The probability that you will win a raffle.

3 The probability that someone prefers apples to bananas.

4 The probability that someone will win a dice game.

5 The probability that the school football team will win 3–1.

6 The probability that you will get home from school on time.

7 The probability that someone has 3 sisters.

We can show probabilities on a **probability scale:**

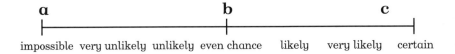

impossible very unlikely unlikely even chance likely very likely certain

a The grass on the school field will turn purple tomorrow.
b If I toss a coin it will land heads up.
c It will be a sunny day in the Sahara desert.

We often draw probability scales with a number scale:

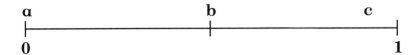

An event that is **impossible** has a **probability of 0**.
An event that is **certain** has a **probability of 1**.

Exercise 15:7

1 Copy this probability scale.

Mark these probabilities on your scale.

a It will snow in Manchester in January.

b It will snow in Manchester in April.

c It will snow in Manchester in August.

2 Copy this probability scale.

Mark these probabilities on your scale.

a You will eat meat tomorrow.

b You will eat bread tomorrow.

c You will eat Christmas cake tomorrow.

3 Copy this probability scale.

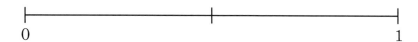

Mark these probabilities on your scale.

a You will run to school.

b You will ride to school.

c You will fly to school.

d You will catch a bus to school.

4 Copy this probability scale.

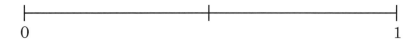

Mark these probabilities on your scale.

a You will get a 4 when you roll a 6-sided dice.

b You will get red on this spinner.

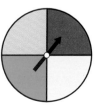

c You will win a raffle with 1 ticket when 200 are sold.

5 Copy this probability scale.

Mark these probabilities on your scale.

You roll a 10-sided dice.

a You get a 5.

b You get an even number.

c You get a number between 1 and 10.

d You get a number between 11 and 20.

1 Robert puts these counters in a bag.

He takes a counter without looking
   a Which colour counter is Robert most likely to pick?
   b Which colour counter is Robert least likely to pick?

2 Caroline puts these counters in a bag.

She takes a counter without looking
   a Which colour counter is Caroline most likely to pick?
   b Which colour counter is Caroline least likely to pick?
   c Caroline wants each colour to have an equally likely chance
        of being picked. Write down the extra counters Caroline needs
        to add to her bag.

3 ⬤⬤⬤⬤⬤ ⬤⬤⬤⬤

These counters are in a bag.
Desmond picks a counter from the same bag **10** times.
He puts it back each time.
   a How many green counters does he expect to get?
   b How many orange counters does he expect to get?

Desmond picks a counter from the same bag **20** times.
   c How many green counters does he expect to get?
   d How many orange counters does he expect to get?

Desmond picks a counter from the same bag **50** times.
   c How many green counters does he expect to get?
   d How many orange counters does he expect to get?

4 Amy rolls this 6-sided dice with these numbers on the faces.

    a Write down the probability she rolls a 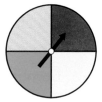.

    b Write down the probability that she rolls a ⚄.

    c Write down the probability she rolls a ⚄.

5 Write down true or false for each statement.

    a Each colour on this spinner has an equal chance of being spun.

    b There is an equal chance of Ryan eating a mud sandwich and a cheese sandwich.

6 **a** Write down the 3 methods for estimating probability.

    b Which method would you use to estimate the probability that it will snow at New Year?

    c Which method would you use to estimate the probability that a train will arrive on time?

7 Copy this probability scale.

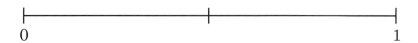

You roll a 10-sided dice.
Mark these probabilities on your probability scale.

    a You roll a 5.

    b You roll a 9.

    c You roll a number between 1 and 8.

16 Percentages

QUESTIONS

The per cent symbol (%) seems to have originated in business.

In the sixteenth century a symbol like a capital Z with a circle at either end was written to represent one one-hundredth.

1 Percentages

About 70% of the surface of the Earth is covered by water.

| **Percentage** | Percentage means out of 100. % is the symbol for percentages. |

Example

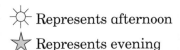

☼ Represents afternoon

⭐ Represents evening

A Year 9 trip is being planned.

100 pupils were asked if they would prefer to have the trip on a Saturday afternoon or Saturday evening.

The diagram shows the 100 replies. Each symbol represents 1 pupil or 1%.

There are 30 ☼ which means 30% chose the afternoon.

The total percentage is 100%.

100% − 30% = 70%
70% chose the evening.

Exercise 16:1

1 The 100 pupils were asked if they would like to go ten-pin bowling. Those that said yes are coloured red.

a How many wanted to go bowling?

b What percentage wanted to go bowling?

c What percentage did not want to go bowling?

Check that your answers for **b** and **c** add up to 100%.

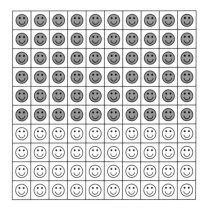

2 The trip would also include a meal.
The 100 pupils were asked if
they would like a pizza.
Pupils wanting pizzas are
coloured yellow.

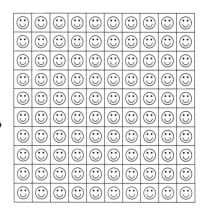

    a How many pupils wanted a pizza?

    b What percentage of pupils
       wanted a pizza?

    c What percentage of pupils did
       not want a pizza?

Check that your answers to **b** and **c**
add up to 100%.

3 The 100 pupils were asked which
pizza they would prefer.
The choice was ham or vegetarian.
Pupils wanting ham are
coloured red. Pupils wanting
vegetarian are coloured green.

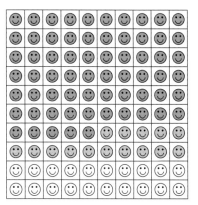

    a What percentage of pupils
       chose ham?

    b What percentage of pupils
       chose vegetarian?

    c What percentage of pupils
       did not choose either?

Check that your answers add up to 100%.

4 A week before the trip, 85% of the pupils going had paid
their money.
What percentage of pupils had not paid their money?

5 To go on the trip all pupils have to return a permission slip.
8% of the permission slips have not been returned.
What percentage of pupils have returned their permission slips?

Example

Here are 100 balloons.

45 out of 100 are red.
45% of the balloons are red.

45% as a fraction is $\dfrac{45}{100}$.

55 out of 100 are blue.
55% of the balloons are blue.

55% as a fraction is $\dfrac{55}{100}$.

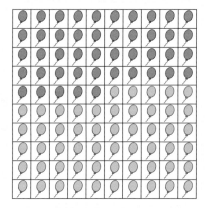

Exercise 16:2

There are 100 balloons in each diagram.

1 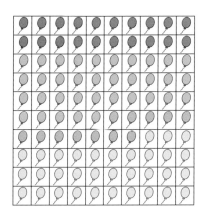   **2**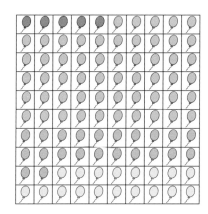

For each diagram,

a Write down the amount coloured red as a   **i** percentage   **ii** fraction.

b Write down the amount coloured blue as a   **i** percentage   **ii** fraction.

c Write down the amount coloured green as a   **i** percentage   **ii** fraction.

d Write down the amount coloured yellow as a   **i** percentage   **ii** fraction.

e Check that the four percentages add up to 100%.

W **1 3** On the worksheet, shade the following amounts.
Write each percentage as a fraction.

    a 12%   **c** 95%   **e** 75%

    b 58%   **d** 32%   **f** 6%

Example   Pie-charts can be used to represent percentages.
The whole pie-chart represents 100%.

This pie-chart is divided into
10 sections.
Each section represents 10%.

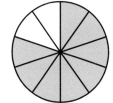

80% is blue.

$\dfrac{80}{100}$ is blue.

20% is white.

$\dfrac{20}{100}$ is white.

---

4   For each pie-chart write down:

  i the percentage that is blue   **iii** the percentage left white

  ii the fraction that is blue   **iv** the fraction left white.

  a   **b**   **c**   **d**

5   Write these percentages as fractions.

  a $23\% = \dfrac{23}{100}$ **d** $91\% = \ldots$ **g** $11\% = \ldots$

  b $43\% = \ldots$ **e** $7\% = \ldots$ **h** $9\% = \ldots$

  c $79\% = \ldots$ **f** $67\% = \ldots$ **i** $41\% = \ldots$

6   Write these fractions as percentages.

  a $\dfrac{38}{100} = 38\%$ **c** $\dfrac{5}{100} = \ldots$ **e** $\dfrac{8}{100} = \ldots$ **g** $\dfrac{16}{100} = \ldots$

  b $\dfrac{77}{100} = \ldots$ **d** $\dfrac{65}{100} = \ldots$ **f** $\dfrac{99}{100} = \ldots$ **h** $\dfrac{44}{100} = \ldots$

In the diagram there are 100 squares.

We can describe this in several ways.

25 squares out of 100 are red.

$\frac{25}{100}$ of the squares are red.

25% of the squares are red.

$\frac{1}{4}$ of the squares are red.

$\frac{1}{4} = 25\%$

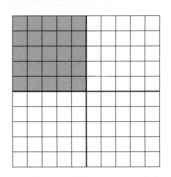

Exercise 16:3

In each diagram there are 100 squares.

1 a How many squares are red?

   b Write this as a percentage.

   $\frac{1}{2}$ of the squares are red.

   c Copy and complete:

      $\frac{1}{2} = \ldots\%$

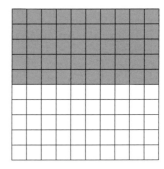

2 a How many squares are red?

   b Write this as a percentage.

   $\frac{3}{4}$ of the squares are red.

   c Copy and complete:

      $\frac{3}{4} = \ldots\%$

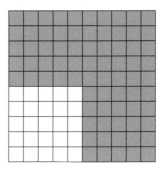

3 In a similar diagram if only one row of squares is red, $\frac{1}{10}$ is red.

   Copy and complete $\frac{1}{10} = \ldots\%$

2   Percentage of an amount

At this party hire shop you need to leave 25% of the cost of an item as a deposit.

You need to learn these fractions and percentages.
Copy them into your book.

$50\% = \dfrac{1}{2}$

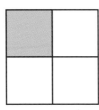

$25\% = \dfrac{1}{4}$

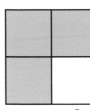

$75\% = \dfrac{3}{4}$

$10\% = \dfrac{1}{10}$

Example   For the school trip a coach is booked.
The cost of hiring the coach is £200.

A deposit of 25% is due. How much is the deposit?

25% is the same as $\dfrac{1}{4}$.

To find $\dfrac{1}{4}$ you have to divide by 4.

$$25\% \text{ of } £200 = \dfrac{1}{4} \text{ of } £200$$
$$= £200 \div 4$$
$$= £50$$

The deposit is £50.

Exercise 16:4

1 To hire the following items, **a deposit of 25%** must be paid.
Work out the deposit.

a  £20

c  £240

e  £120

b  £400

d 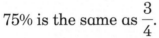 £16 for 200

f  £80

Example Mrs Smart owns a clothes shop.
She pays the wholesaler 75% of
the selling price.

Mrs Smart sells a T-shirt for £16.
How much does she pay the wholesaler?

To find 75% of £16.

75% is the same as $\frac{3}{4}$.

First find $\frac{1}{4}$ of £16 by dividing by 4.

$$\frac{1}{4} \text{ of } £16 = £16 \div 4$$
$$= £4$$

Then find $\frac{3}{4}$ by multiplying this answer by 3.

$$\frac{3}{4} \text{ of } £16 = 3 \times £4$$
$$= £12$$

The wholesaler receives £12.

---

2 How much does the wholesaler receive for each of these articles?

a $\frac{1}{4}$ of £24 $= £24 \div 4$

$= £...$

$\frac{3}{4}$ of £24 $= 3 \times ...$

$= £...$

£24

b $\frac{1}{4}$ of £20 $= ...$

$= £...$

$\frac{3}{4}$ of £20 $= 3 \times ...$

$= £...$

£20

3 How much does the wholesaler receive for each of these articles?

a

£8

c

£36

b

£40

d

£32

Sports shop prices are reduced by 10%.

10% is the same as $\frac{1}{10}$.

Example   Julie is buying sports equipment and prices are reduced by 10%.
How much will Julie pay for a tennis racket that was £40?

$$10\% \text{ of } £40 = \frac{1}{10} \text{ of } £40$$
$$= £40 \div 10$$
$$= £4$$

Reduction $= £4$

Sale price $= £40 - £4$
$$= £36$$

H 2   **4**   For each of these articles,
  i how much is the 10% reduction
  ii what is the sale price?

a    £60

c   £10

b    £20

d    £200

5 i Find the percentage given.
  ii Reduce the prices by that amount

a 10% of £80	**d** 25% of 100	**g** 10% of £300
b 25% of £20	**e** 10% of £400	**h** 25% of £80
c 50% of £12	**f** 50% of £30	**i** 75% of £80

G 1, 2, 3

1, 2, 3

Once you can find 10% of an amount, you can easily find other percentages.

Example

a Find 30% of £40.

b Find 5% of £60.

First find 10% of £40.

$$10\% \text{ of } £40 = \frac{1}{10} \text{ of } £40$$
$$= £40 \div 10$$
$$= £4$$

First find 10% of £60.

$$10\% \text{ of } £60 = \frac{1}{10} \text{ of } £60$$
$$= £60 \div 10$$
$$= £6$$

30% is three times 10%.

$$10\% \text{ of } £40 = £4$$
$$30\% \text{ of } £40 = 3 \times £4$$
$$= £12$$

5% is half of 10%.

$$10\% \text{ of } £60 = £6$$
$$5\% \text{ of } £60 = £6 \div 2$$
$$= £3$$

Exercise 16:5

W 2, 3

1 **a** Find 10% of £60.
   b Find 30% of £60.
   c Find 5% of £60.

2 **a** Find 10% of £80.
   b Find 70% of £80.
   c Find 5% of £80.

3 **a** Find 10% of £200.
   b Find 40% of £200.
   c Find 5% of £200.

4 **a** Find 10% of £20.
   b Find 60% of £20.
   c Find 90% of £20.

5 Find 80% of £30.

6 Find 20% of £5.

7 Find 30% of £90.

Example   Pavneet gets £24 a week for his Saturday job in a clothes shop.
The shopkeeper is going to increase Pavneet's money by 10%.
How much extra will he get?

Find 10% of £24.

$$10\% \text{ of } £24 = \frac{1}{10} \text{ of } £24$$
$$= £24 \div 10$$
$$= £2.40$$

As we are using money we must always write our answers to 2 decimals even if the last figure is zero.

Exercise 16:6

1 Yvonne gets £16 for her paper round.
She is given a 10% pay rise.
How much extra will she get?

2 Clive works in a garden centre and is normally paid £4 an hour.
On a Sunday he is paid 50% more.
How much is he paid an hour on a Sunday?

3 Jason bought a pair of trainers reduced in a sale by 10%.
The original price was £65.
How much did Jason save?

4 Video tapes cost £2 each. If you buy ten tapes you get 10% discount.
How much would you save on each video tape?

5 Work out the following discounts on £12
    a 10%   **b** 20%   **c** 30%   **d** 40%

3 Percentages, fractions and decimals

* *

Examples   Work out by multiplication

1   In the diagram, 35% is shaded blue.

As a fraction this is $\dfrac{35}{100}$.

This can also be written as a decimal:

3 **5** **÷** **1** **0** **0** **=**   [*0.35*]

$35\% = \dfrac{35}{100} = 0.35$

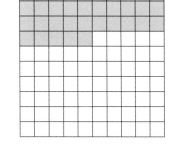

2   In the diagram, 6% is shaded blue.

As a fraction this is $\dfrac{6}{100}$.

This can also be written as a decimal:

6 **÷** **1** **0** **0** **=**   [*0.06*]

$6\% = \dfrac{6}{100} = 0.06$

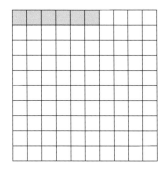

Exercise 16:7

Write each of these percentages as:
a a fraction of 100   **b** a decimal.
The first one is done for you.

1 $17\% = \dfrac{17}{100} = 0.17$ **5** $23\% = \ldots = \ldots$

2 $85\% = \ldots = \ldots$ **6** $5\% = \ldots = \ldots$

3 $42\% = \ldots = \ldots$ **7** $64\% = \ldots = \ldots$

4 $7\% = \ldots = \ldots$ **8** $2\% = \ldots = \ldots$

4   **9** Fill in the gaps in the table.

	Percentage	Fraction	Decimal
a	45%	...	...
b	...%	$\frac{23}{100}$	...
c	...%	...	0.56
d	5%	...	...
e	...%	$\frac{7}{100}$	...
f	...%	...	0.04
g	...%	$\frac{15}{100}$	...

1   The diagram shows the weather on 100 days during the winter.
    Each symbol represents 1 day.

 represents sunny.

 represents cloudy.

represents rainy.

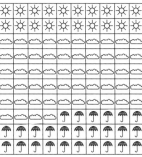

a What percentage of the days were sunny?
b What percentage of the days were cloudy?
c What percentage of the days were rainy?

2   In a survey, 15% of the people asked owned a dog?
    What percentage of the people asked did not own a dog?

3   In the pie chart, each section represents 10%.

    Write down:
    a the percentage shaded blue.
    b the fraction shaded blue.
    c the percentage left white.
    d the fraction left white.

4   Write these as fractions. The first one is done for you.

    a $14\% = \dfrac{14}{100}$ b 9%   c 95%   d 3%   e 64%

5   Write these fractions as percentages.
    a $\dfrac{62}{100}$ b $\dfrac{17}{100}$ c $\dfrac{8}{100}$ d $\dfrac{91}{100}$ e $\dfrac{1}{100}$

6   Write these fractions as percentages.
    a $\dfrac{1}{2}$ b $\dfrac{3}{4}$ c $\dfrac{1}{10}$ d $\dfrac{1}{4}$

7   Find 50% of: a £6   b £42   c £50

8   Find 25% of: a £100   b £60   c £84

9   Find 10% of: a £90   b £120   c £40

10 In a sale the price of a TV is reduced by 25%.
The original price is £80.

   a What is the reduction?

   b What is the sale price?

11 Chris works in a garden centre.
He earns £250 a week. He is given a pay
rise of 10%.

   a How much extra will he get?

   b How much will he earn in a week
after the rise?

12 **a** Find 10% of £20.

   b Find 30% of £90.

   c Find 5% of £90.

13 Natalie books a holiday to Spain costing £285.
She pays a deposit of 10%.
How much is the deposit?

14 Copy the table and fill in the gaps.

	Percentage	Fraction	Decimal
a	9%	...	...
b	...%	$\frac{43}{100}$	...
c	...%	...	0.12

QUESTIONS

You plot co-ordinates using x and y axes.

Computers can plot graphs using 3 dimensions.

This is a graph of $z = \sin xy$.

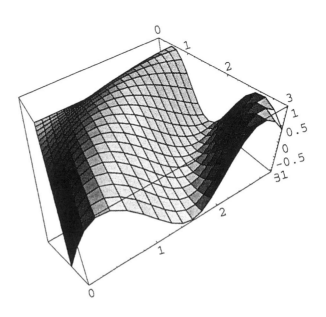

1   Co-ordinates

We use co-ordinates
to find the position
of a point.

Axes	We draw two lines. These are called **axes**.

x axis	The horizontal line (across) is called the **x axis**.

y axis	The vertical line (up) is called the **y axis**.

The co-ordinates of the
point P are $(3, 2)$. Put your finger on O.
Trace your finger across the x axis to the 3.
Then go up the line until you come to P, which is
level with the 2 on the y axis.
The position of the point P is $(3, 2)$.

x co-ordinate	The first number is the **x co-ordinate**.

y co-ordinate	The second number is the **y co-ordinate**.

$$(3, 2)$$

x co-ordinate   y co-ordinate

The point Q has co-ordinates $(0, 3)$.
You do not need to go across the
x axis because the x co-ordinate is 0.
Just go up the y axis to the 3.
The position of the point Q is $(0, 3)$.

Exercise 17:1

This picture shows the planets orbiting around the Sun.
Check that the co-ordinates of the Sun are

Across   Up
(5,   6)

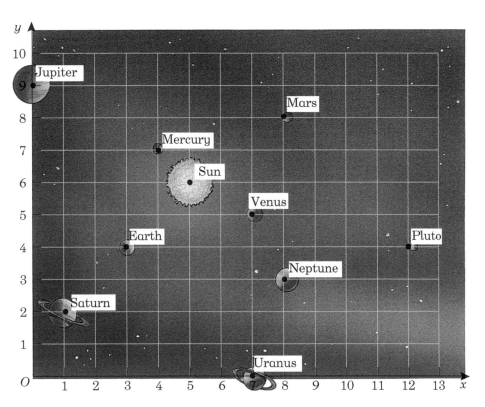

1 Write down the planet with co-ordinates:

   a (3, 4)   **d** (12, 4)

   b (7, 5)   **e** (4, 7)

   c (1, 2)   **f** (0, 9)

2 Write down the co-ordinates of these planets.
   Remember:
   i across first, then up
   ii put a comma between the numbers
   iii add brackets.

   a Earth   **d** Venus

   b Mars   **e** Uranus

   c Jupiter   **f** Neptune

Exercise 17:2

This is a map of the planet Mars in 2100AD.

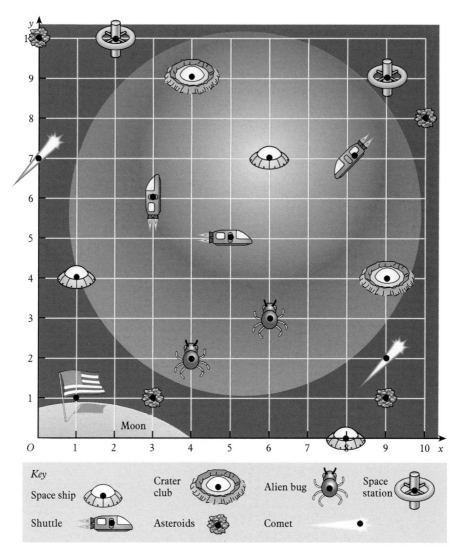

1   There is a space ship at (1, 4).
    Write down the co-ordinates of two more space ships.

2   Write down what is at the point with co-ordinates.
    a (4, 2)   **c** (6, 3)   **e** (0, 7)
    b (3, 6)   **d** (9, 9)   **f** (4, 9)

3   Write down the co-ordinates of these things:
    a the moon flag   **b** two comets   **c** all 4 asteroids.

4   Activity: Fill in your own map of Mars.
    Make a key. List the features with their co-ordinates.

Example

a Copy these axes on to squared paper.

b Plot the points with a cross. Join them as you go.

$(5, 1) \rightarrow (4, 2) \rightarrow$
$(2, 4) \rightarrow (1, 6) \rightarrow$
$(1, 7) \rightarrow (3, 9) \rightarrow (5, 7)$

c Join the point $(5, 10)$ to the point $(5, 0)$ with a dotted line. Reflect your shape in the dotted line. This is the **mirror line**.

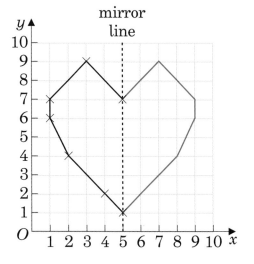

Exercise 17:3

 1 Draw the picture in the example for yourself. Use a sharp pencil and ruler to join the points.

2 a Draw another set of axes like the ones in question **1**.

b Plot the points with a cross. Join them in order as you go.

$(5, 1) \rightarrow (6, 3) \rightarrow (8, 6) \rightarrow (6, 9) \rightarrow (5, 11)$

c Join the point $(5, 11)$ to the point $(5, 0)$ with a dotted line. Reflect your shape in the dotted line.

3 a Draw another set of axes like the ones in question **1**.

b Plot the points with a cross. Join them in order as you go.

$(5, 1) \rightarrow (4, 1) \rightarrow (5, 4) \rightarrow$
$(3, 2) \rightarrow (2, 3) \rightarrow (2, 6) \rightarrow$
$(7, 8) \rightarrow (5, 10)$

c Join the points $(5, 11)$ to $(5, 1)$ with a dotted line. Reflect your shape in the dotted line.

4 a Draw another set of axes like the ones in question **1**.

b Plot the points with a cross.
Join them in order as you go.
$(5,1) \rightarrow (6,1) \rightarrow (5,3) \rightarrow$
$(6,2) \rightarrow (7,2) \rightarrow (8,3) \rightarrow$
$(8,5) \rightarrow (7,6) \rightarrow (5,5) \rightarrow$
$(7,7) \rightarrow (7,9) \rightarrow (5,10)$

c Join the point $(5, 11)$ to the point $(5, 1)$ with a dotted line.
Reflect your shape in the dotted line.

5 This is a code.
Each pair of co-ordinates will give you a letter.

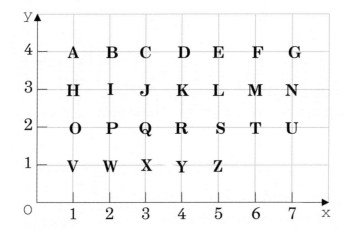

a Check that $(3, 4)$ stands for the letter C.
Check that the letter S is at $(5, 2)$.

b The sets of co-ordinates stand for words.
Can you decode them?
i $(3,4)$ $(5,3)$ $(7,2)$ $(2,4)$
ii $(1,3)$ $(5,4)$ $(1,4)$ $(4,2)$ $(6,2)$ $(5,2)$
iii $(2,4)$ $(4,2)$ $(2,3)$ $(4,4)$ $(7,4)$ $(5,4)$
iv $(2,2)$ $(1,4)$ $(3,4)$ $(4,3)$ | $(1,2)$ $(6,4)$ | $(3,4)$
$(1,4)$ $(4,2)$ $(4,4)$ $(5,2)$

c Write the codes for NIM, SNAP, OTHELLO, HANGMAN.

d Think of some games yourself. Write their letters in code.

2 Patterns in co-ordinates

Anthony is playing a co-ordinate game.

Anthony has a set of co-ordinate cards.
He notices that the co-ordinates
make a number pattern.
Look at the co-ordinates.
What do you notice?

The *x* co-ordinate is 1 more than
the *y* co-ordinate on each card.
This is the **rule** for this set of cards.

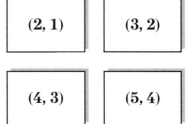

(2, 1)   (3, 2)

(4, 3)   (5, 4)

Exercise 17:4

1 Draw 4 more cards that could belong to Anthony's set.
Remember, they must follow the rule for this set of cards.

2 a These are Karl's cards:
Look at the co-ordinates.
What do you notice?
What is the rule?

b Draw 4 more cards that follow
Karl's rule.

(1, 1)   (3, 3)

(7, 7)   (10, 10)

3 a These are Nicola's cards:
Look at the co-ordinates.
What do you notice?
What is the rule?

b Draw 4 more cards that follow
Nicola's rule.

(2, 4)   (6, 12)

(3, 6)   (4, 8)

3 a These are Hayley's cards:
Look at the co-ordinates.
What do you notice?
What is the rule?

b Draw 4 more cards that follow
Hayley's rule.

Example   Look for a pattern in these co-ordinates.
Use the pattern to find the missing co-ordinates.

	x *y*	
These are the *x* co-ordinates. You add 1 each time. The next *x* co-ordinates are **6** and **7**.	(2 , 8) (3 , 7) → (4 , 6) ← (5 , 5) (... , ...) (... , ...)	These are the *y* co-ordinates. You take away 1 each time. The next *y* co-ordinates are 4 and 3.

The missing co-ordinates are (**6**, **4**) and (**7**, **3**).

Look for a pattern in these co-ordinates.
Use the pattern to find the missing co-ordinates.

5 (4 , 3)
(5 , 4)
(6 , 5)
(7 , 6)
(... , ...)
(... , ...)

7 (3 , 0)
(5 , 2)
(7 , 4)
(9 , 6)
(... , ...)
(... , ...)

9 (3 , 1)
(6 , 1)
(9 , 1)
(12, 1)
(... , ...)
(... , ...)

6 (2 , 3)
(4 , 4)
(6 , 5)
(8 , 6)
(... , ...)
(... , ...)

8 (5 , 10)
(10, 8)
(15, 6)
(20, 4)
(... , ...)
(... , ...)

10 (4 , 9)
(4 , 8)
(4 , 7)
(4 , 6)
(... , ...)
(... , ...)

Sometimes we find a pattern when we *add* the co-ordinates together.

Example   Look at these co-ordinates $(1, 4)$ $(3, 2)$ $(0, 5)$.

    a What do you notice when you add the x and y co-ordinates together?

    b Use your pattern to fill in the missing numbers of these co-ordinates

        $(4, \ldots)$ $(5, \ldots)$ $(\ldots, 3)$

    a The two numbers add up to 5
        $1 + 4 = 5$ $3 + 2 = 5$ $0 + 5 = 5$

    b The missing numbers are $(4, 1)$, $(5, 0)$, $(2, 3)$.

For each set of co-ordinates, look for a pattern. Use the pattern to find the missing co-ordinates.

11 **a** $(3, 3)$, $(0, 6)$, $(2, 4)$, $(5, \ldots)$, $(4, \ldots)$

    b $(6, 4)$, $(8, 2)$, $(2, 8)$, $(7, \ldots)$, $(2, \ldots)$, $(\ldots, 9)$

    c $(5, 7)$, $(6, 6)$, $(8, 4)$, $(2, \ldots)$, $(12, \ldots)$, $(\ldots, 1)$

    d $(3, 12)$, $(5, 10)$, $(7, 8)$, $(\ldots, 5)$, $(0, \ldots)$, $(\ldots, 9)$

    e $(12, 8)$, $(13, 7)$, $(18, 2)$, $(15, \ldots)$, $(\ldots, 10)$, $(17, \ldots)$

Exercise 17:5

W 2

In these questions the patterns have been drawn on the grid.

1

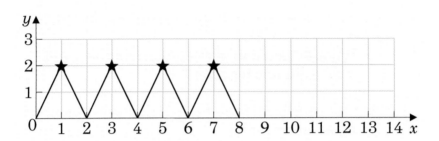

Continue the triangle pattern to the end of the grid.
Mark a star ★ at the point of each triangle.
The co-ordinates of the first star are $(1, 2)$.

a Write down the co-ordinates of the first five stars.

b What are the co-ordinates of the 7th star?

c What are the co-ordinates of the 10th star?

2

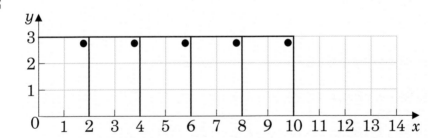

Continue the tiling pattern to the end of the grid.
Mark a dot ● at the corner of each tile to follow the pattern.

a Write down the co-ordinates of the first 5 dots.

b What are the co-ordinates of the 7th dot?

c What are the co-ordinates of the 10th dot?

1 a

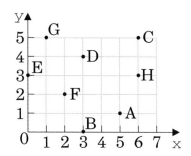

Write down the letter with co-ordinates:

i $(3, 0)$

ii $(6, 5)$

iii $(1, 5)$

iv $(2, 2)$

b Write down the co-ordinates of these letters:

i A **ii** D **iii** E **iv** H

2 a Draw a set of axes like the one in question **1**.

b Plot the points.
Join them in order as you go.
$(4, 1) \rightarrow (1, 1) \rightarrow (3, 3) \rightarrow (1, 4) \rightarrow (4, 4)$

c Join the point $(4, 5)$ to $(4, 0)$ with a dotted line.
Reflect your shape in the doted line.

3 This is a code.
Each pair of co-ordinates will
give you a letter.
The sets of co-ordinates stand
for words. Can you decode them?

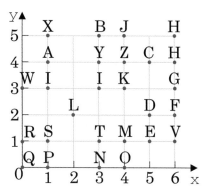

a $(1, 1)\ (4, 3)\ (1, 3)$

b $(4, 1)\ (4, 0)\ (1, 0)\ (5, 1)\ (5, 2)$

c $(5, 4)\ (1, 4)\ (0, 1)$

d $(3, 5)\ (4, 1)\ (1, 5)$

e Write the code for BICYCLE.

f Write the code for TRAIN.

4 These are Kamal's cards.

   a Look at the co-ordinates.
      What do you notice?

   b What is the rule?

   c Draw 4 more cards that follow
      Kamal's rule.

(2, 3)	(4, 5)
(1, 2)	(8, 9)

5 Look for a pattern in these co-ordinates.
Use the pattern to find the missing co-ordinates.

a (3 , 4)
   (3 , 5)
   (3 , 6)
   (3 , 7)
   (......, ...)
   (......, ...)

c (4 , 2)
   (6 , 3)
   (8 , 4)
   (10 , 5)
   (......, ...)
   (......, ...)

b (2 , 8)
   (3 , 8)
   (4 , 8)
   (5 , 8)
   (......, ...)
   (......, ...)

d (3 , 5)
   (5 , 7)
   (7 , 9)
   (9 , 11)
   (......, ...)
   (......, ...)

6 For each set of co-ordinates, look for a pattern when you add the
x and y co-ordinates together.
Use the pattern to find the missing co-ordinates.

   a (2, 3), (3, 2), (0, 5), (..., 0), (1, ...) (4, ...)

   b (4, 3), (5, 2), (7, 0), (..., 7), (6, ...), (3, ...)

   c (5, 10), (11, 4), (1, 14), (7, ...), (6, ...), (..., 12)

   d (4, 13), (16, 1), (3, 14), (2, ...), (..., 7), (9, ...)

   e (12, 12), (11, 13), (10, 14), (9, ...), (20, ...), (..., 1)

18 More fun

1 Fruit machine

This fruit machine has three reels.

Each reel has pictures of fruit on it.

You are going to design your own fruit machine.

Here is a simple one to start you off.
You will use strips for the reels.
It has just two reels.
Each reel has three fruits.
Here are the fruits that are on each reel.

The only way to win on this machine is to get two plums.

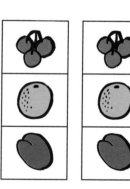

W 1, 2 **1** You need worksheets 1 and 2.
Cut out the strips from worksheet 1.
Cut out the slots from worksheet 2.
Fit the strips into the first two reels of the fruit machine.

2 Start with 🍒 in both windows.

You are now going to list all the different ways the machine could stop.

W 3   **3**   Copy this table:

Reel 1	Reel 2
Cherries	Cherries
Cherries	
Cherries	

You need 6 more rows.

4   Move reel 2 one space up. Fill in the next row of your table.

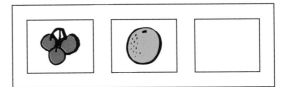

5   Move reel 2 again. Fill in the next row of your table.

6   Move reel 1 one space up.

Put reel 2 back to .

Fill in the next row of your table.

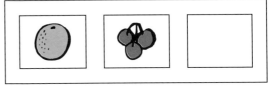

7   Carry on until you have filled in the rest of your table.

8   How many different ways can the machine stop?

9   What is the probability of winning?

W 4,5,6   **10**   Now design your own fruit machines. You could:
- Have more fruits.
- Use three reels.
- Have more prizes.
- Put the same fruit on a reel more than once.

Write down what you choose.

   a   Work out how many ways the machine can stop.

   b   Work out the probability of winning.

2 Running a disco!

You have been asked to help organise a disco at the local Youth Club.

These are some of the jobs you'll need to do:

- Work out the cost of the tickets so that you do not make a loss. You may want to make a profit.

- Organise a buffet so that there is enough food.

- Choose a good DJ for the evening.

- Organise publicity and printing of the tickets.

- Pay some cleaners to tidy up when it's over.

YOUTH CLUB DISCO
FRIDAY 14th FEBRUARY

The price of the disco tickets depends on how much you spend on organising it.

You need to work out some costs:

Expenses
- The hall will hold 100 people. It is free.
- The local DJ charges £60 for the evening.
- The publicity and printing of the tickets costs £30.
- The cleaners will charge £20.

Use Worksheet 7 to work out how much money there will be to spend on refreshments. This will be the **balance** after expenses. You must know the most and the least money in hand before you can start to choose and pay for the buffet food.

 Use Worksheet 8 to decide what you will order for the buffet.

The caterers have sent you a large choice of snacks.

- Fill in the cost per 100 portions.
- Choose 8 different items from their list.
- Add up the cost for 100 portions.
- Fill in the end column of the table on Worksheet 8.

1 Use your data on Worksheet 8 to answer the questions on Worksheet 7.

2 Make a list of other jobs that will need to be done for a successful evening.

3 Can you think of any problems that might result in a big loss instead of a profit?
Write them down.

4 Make a design for one of these:
- Publicity poster
- Ticket
- Menu

You may be able to use a computer.

3   Planning a bedroom

Daisy is planning a bedroom.
She wants to fit in

- a bed

- a wardrobe

- a desk

- a chest of drawers

- a bookcase

- a chair.

Exercise 18:1

W9, 10   **1**   Cut out the shapes from the worksheet.

2   Arrange them on the plan.
Think about where they go – don't block the door! Don't put a
wardrobe in front of the window!

3   Stick them on the plan.

4   Write a sentence saying why you arranged the bedroom
that way.

Exercise 18:2

Now you have more choice.

 11

1   Cut out the shapes from the worksheet.

2   Arrange them on the plan.
    Choose which you want carefully.

3   Stick them on the plan.

4   Write a sentence saying why you chose that furniture.

Exercise 18:3

Now make your bedroom plan more interesting.

1   Choose a colour scheme. Get samples of paint colours and
    wallpaper designs.

2   Find pictures of furniture and bedding designs in magazines.
    Cut them out and make a display.

3   Write about your design choice.

+ add total sum plus +

Exercise 1

Work out the answers in your head.

1 13 + 7

2 The sum of 8 and 6

3 23 plus 22

4 19 + 4

5 The total of 12 and 18

6 41 + 7

7 The sum of 11 and 16

8 53 + 5

9 21 + 34

10 The total of 60 and 20

Exercise 2

1
```
  4 6
+   3
-----
```

2
```
    9
+   3
-----
```

3
```
  1 3
+   9
-----
```

4
```
  4 4
+ 1 8
-----
```

5
```
  7 6 2
+ 1 3 4
-------
```

6
```
  2 4 5
+   1 6
-------
```

7
```
  5 4
+ 3 2
-----
```

8
```
    7
+   7
-----
```

9
```
    7
+ 2 7
-----
```

10
```
  3 2
+ 1 9
-----
```

11
```
  5 4 2
+ 1 3 6
-------
```

12
```
  3 8 7
+   2 4
-------
```

13
```
  4 0 1
+   4 8
-------
```

14
```
    8
+   6
-----
```

15
```
  3 8
+   6
-----
```

16
```
  5 7
+ 3 3
-----
```

17
```
  2 1 4
+ 6 3 5
-------
```

18
```
  2 6 8
+ 1 7 3
-------
```

– take away subtract minus difference –

Exercise 3

Work out the answers in your head.

1 9 take away 5

2 10 − 3

3 15 − 4

4 23 minus 2

5 30 − 10

6 Subtract 5 from 17

7 24 − 11

8 The difference between 12 and 18

9 68 − 22

10 21 take away 3

Exercise 4

1
$$\begin{array}{r} 8 \\ -\ 3 \\ \hline \end{array}$$

2
$$\begin{array}{r} 8\ 5 \\ -2\ 3 \\ \hline \end{array}$$

3
$$\begin{array}{r} 3\ 4\ 5 \\ -1\ 2\ 3 \\ \hline \end{array}$$

4
$$\begin{array}{r} 2\ 1 \\ -\ \ 9 \\ \hline \end{array}$$

5
$$\begin{array}{r} 3\ 6 \\ -1\ 8 \\ \hline \end{array}$$

6
$$\begin{array}{r} 5\ 3\ 2 \\ -1\ 2\ 7 \\ \hline \end{array}$$

7
$$\begin{array}{r} 1\ 6 \\ -\ \ 5 \\ \hline \end{array}$$

8
$$\begin{array}{r} 4\ 6 \\ -1\ 5 \\ \hline \end{array}$$

9
$$\begin{array}{r} 7\ 5\ 6 \\ -2\ 4\ 5 \\ \hline \end{array}$$

10
$$\begin{array}{r} 3\ 2 \\ -\ \ 8 \\ \hline \end{array}$$

11
$$\begin{array}{r} 4\ 3 \\ -2\ 9 \\ \hline \end{array}$$

12
$$\begin{array}{r} 4\ 2\ 1 \\ -2\ 9\ 9 \\ \hline \end{array}$$

13
$$\begin{array}{r} 2\ 7 \\ -\ \ 4 \\ \hline \end{array}$$

14
$$\begin{array}{r} 6\ 7 \\ -2\ 4 \\ \hline \end{array}$$

15
$$\begin{array}{r} 8\ 6\ 9 \\ -4\ 6\ 3 \\ \hline \end{array}$$

16
$$\begin{array}{r} 1\ 4\ 3 \\ -\ \ 1\ 6 \\ \hline \end{array}$$

17
$$\begin{array}{r} 5\ 2 \\ -\ 3\ 6 \\ \hline \end{array}$$

18
$$\begin{array}{r} 3\ 0\ 4 \\ -1\ 8\ 8 \\ \hline \end{array}$$

333

× multiply   times   product ×

Exercise 5

Work out the answers in your head.

1 3×6

2 Multiply 7 by 5

3 10 times 4

4 8×3

5 The product of 2 and 9

6 4×20

7 Multiply 11 by 6

8 5×5

9 21 times 3

10 The product of 5 and 6

Exercise 6

1
```
    2
×   8
────
```

2
```
  8 5
×   3
────
```

3
```
    7
×   4
────
```

4
```
  3 2
×   3
────
```

5
```
  1 4
×   2
────
```

6
```
  2 1
×   4
────
```

7
```
  1 5
×   3
────
```

8
```
  2 3
×   4
────
```

9
```
  3 4 6
×     2
──────
```

10
```
  3 6
×   4
────
```

11
```
  4 3
×   5
────
```

12
```
  2 5 4
×     3
──────
```

13
```
  5 6
× 1 0
────
```

14
```
  4 7
× 2 0
────
```

15
```
  2 4
× 3 0
────
```

16 33×21

17 44×32

18 26×52

19 35×43

20 56×34

÷ **divide**   **share** ÷

Exercise 7

1 $\dfrac{20}{4}$

2 Divide 21 by 3

3 $36 \div 3$

4 $\dfrac{82}{2}$

5 Share 48 between 4

6 $\dfrac{18}{6}$

7 Divide 42 by 3

8 $32 \div 2$

9 Share 72 between 4

10 $65 \div 5$

Exercise 8

1 $2\overline{)46}$

2 $5\overline{)15}$

3 $4\overline{)52}$

4 $5\overline{)605}$

5 $4\overline{)612}$

6 $10\overline{)250}$

7 $4\overline{)48}$

8 $6\overline{)24}$

9 $3\overline{)72}$

10 $7\overline{)847}$

11 $3\overline{)725}$

12 $10\overline{)470}$

13 $3\overline{)96}$

14 $9\overline{)27}$

15 $6\overline{)84}$

16 $6\overline{)966}$

17 $5\overline{)715}$

18 $10\overline{)830}$

+ addition of decimals +

Set your work out in columns.
Line up the decimal points.

Example

a 2.4 + 3.8

4 + 8 = **12**   2.4   2.4
Write the **2** and   + 3.8   ⟶   2 + 3 + 1 = **6**   + 3.8
carry the **1**   6.2   6.2
                         1   1

b 4.76 + 1.5

Line up the decimal points.   4.76
Write a **0** in the space   + 1.50
Add, starting on the right   6.26
                                  1

Exercise 9

Calculate the answers.

1	5.3 + 4.4	**5**	6.8 + 1.4	**9**	12.5 + 3.94	**13**	4.5 + 1.3

14 23.4 + 14.2

| **2** | 2.8
+ 5.1 | **6** | 2.37
+ 1.24 | **10** | 5.36
+ 21.46 | **15** | 32.4 + 5.3 |

16 6.8 + 23.1

| **3** | 4.26
+ 3.12 | **7** | 7.46
+ 1.82 | **11** | 16.8
+ 5.19 | **17** | 3.9 + 1.5 |

18 11.7 + 7.6

| **4** | 5.61
+ 3.2 | **8** | 6.35
+ 3.8 | **12** | 72.46
+ 19.4 | **19** | 3.4 + 18.5 |

20 4.78 + 2.4

Set your work out in columns.
Line up the decimal points.

Example

a 1.76 − 1.5

Line up the decimal points.
Write a **0** in the space.
Subtract each column, starting on the right.

$$
\begin{array}{r}
1.76 \\
-1.50 \\
\hline
0.26 \\
\end{array}
$$

b 5.27 − 3.81

First $\quad$ 5.27 $\quad$ Next 2 − 8
7 − 1 = 6 $\;$ − 3.81 $\;$ is not possible.

$$
\begin{array}{r}
5.27 \\
-3.81 \\
\hline
.6 \\
\end{array}
$$

Next 2 − 8
is not possible.
Borrow one from
the column to
the left.
12 − 8 = 4

$$
\begin{array}{r}
{}^4\cancel{5}.{}^1 27 \\
-3.81 \\
\hline
.46 \\
\end{array}
$$

Lastly
4 − 3 = 6

$$
\begin{array}{r}
{}^4\cancel{5}.{}^1 27 \\
-3.81 \\
\hline
1.46 \\
\end{array}
$$
Answer

Exercise 10

Find the answers.

1
$$
\begin{array}{r}
8.7 \\
-1.5 \\
\hline
\end{array}
$$

2
$$
\begin{array}{r}
6.9 \\
-2.4 \\
\hline
\end{array}
$$

3
$$
\begin{array}{r}
9.85 \\
-7.02 \\
\hline
\end{array}
$$

4
$$
\begin{array}{r}
5.61 \\
-1.4 \\
\hline
\end{array}
$$

5
$$
\begin{array}{r}
7.2 \\
-3.8 \\
\hline
\end{array}
$$

6
$$
\begin{array}{r}
5.18 \\
-2.91 \\
\hline
\end{array}
$$

7
$$
\begin{array}{r}
8.54 \\
-3.06 \\
\hline
\end{array}
$$

8
$$
\begin{array}{r}
6.9 \\
-4.15 \\
\hline
\end{array}
$$

9
$$
\begin{array}{r}
23.7 \\
-12 \\
\hline
\end{array}
$$

10
$$
\begin{array}{r}
31.6 \\
-7.3 \\
\hline
\end{array}
$$

11
$$
\begin{array}{r}
15.4 \\
-11.25 \\
\hline
\end{array}
$$

12
$$
\begin{array}{r}
6.35 \\
-3.8 \\
\hline
\end{array}
$$

13 2.8 − 1.4

14 4.26 − 3.12

15 7.4 − 1.8

16 4.26 − 2.1

17 17.5 − 3.4

18 6.35 − 3.8

19 9.8 − 2.45

20 26.4 − 3.32

Multiplying by 10

When we **multiply by 10**, all the digits move across **one** column to the **left**.
This makes the number 10 times bigger.

Example

a $34 \times 10 = 340$

H	T	U
	3	4
×10	×10	
3	4	0

b $2.5 \times 10 = 25$

T	U	.	t
	2	.	5
×10	×10		
2	5	.	

Multiplying by 100

When we **multiply by 100**, all the digits move across **two** columns to the **left**.
This makes the number 100 times bigger.

Example

a $86 \times 100 = 8600$

Th	H	T	U
		8	6
	×100	×100	
8	6	0	0

b $3.24 \times 100 = 324$

H	T	U	.	t	h
		3	.	2	4
	×100	×100	×100		
3	2	4			

Exercise 11

Multiply these numbers by 10.

1 42		**11** 3.5
2 56		**12** 7.4
3 78		**13** 10.0
4 21		**14** 24.2
5 35		**15** 2.56
6 234		**16** 16.7
7 612		**17** 4.0
8 723		**18** 0.5
9 817		**19** 0.75
10 389		**20** 7.50

Exercise 12

Multiply these numbers by 100.

1 24		**11** 3.4
2 59		**12** 6.2
3 92		**13** 5.62
4 81		**14** 7.05
5 40		**15** 37.6
6 285		**16** 29.2
7 822		**17** 60.01
8 673		**18** 44.44
9 706		**19** 10.00
10 300		**20** 70.10

Exercise 13

Copy these sums into your book.
Write down the answers.

1 64×10

2 15×100

3 55×100

4 88×10

5 32×10

6 994×10

7 526×100

8 800×10

9 307×100

10 20×10

Dividing by 10

When we **divide by 10**, all the digits move across **one** column to the **right**.
This makes the number smaller.

Example

a $420 \div 10 = 42$

```
H   T   U
4   2   0
 ÷10  ÷10
    4   2
```

Here are some more examples.

b
```
T   U
5   0      50 ÷ 10 = 5
 ÷10
    5
```

c
```
H   T   U  .  t   h
4   2   3  .  9
 ÷10  ÷10  ÷10  ÷10
    4   2  .  3   9
```

$$423.9 \div 10 = 42.39$$

Dividing by 100

When we **divide by 100**, all the digits move across **two** columns to the **right**. This is because $100 = 10 \times 10$. So dividing by 100 is like dividing by 10 twice.

Example

a $5100 \div 100 =$

```
Th   H   T   U
5    1   0   0
  ÷100  ÷100
        5   1
```

Here are some more examples.

b
```
Th   H   T   U
6    9   0   0    6900 ÷ 100 = 69
  ÷100  ÷100
        6   9
```

c
```
Th   H   T   U  .  t   h   th
1    0   6   4  .  6
  ÷100 ÷100 ÷100 ÷100 ÷100
        1   0  .  6   4   6
```

$$1064.6 \div 100 = 10.646$$

Exercise 14

Divide these numbers by 10.

1 230		**9** 3.5
2 80		**10** 35.6
3 750		**11** 322.1
4 2690		**12** 9.9
5 70		**13** 999.9
6 510		**14** 16.1
7 9460		**15** 200.5
8 820		**16** 10.0

Exercise 15

Divide these numbers by 100.

1 6300		**9** 100
2 7800		**10** 764
3 5200		**11** 76.4
4 8100		**12** 99.8
5 3400		**13** 42.39
6 9900		**14** 670.1
7 2500		**15** 700.01
8 1700		**16** 2.7

Exercise 16

Work these out.

1 $750 \div 10$

2 $5500 \div 100$

3 $1100 \div 100$

4 $460 \div 10$

5 $800 \div 100$

6 $90 \div 10$

7 $2460 \div 10$

8 $2800 \div 100$

fractions

Exercise 17

Write down in figures
a the green fraction
b the yellow fraction.

1

2

3
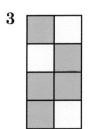

4
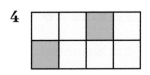

5

6
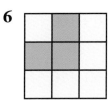

Exercise 18

Write down in words
a the green fraction
b the yellow fraction.

1
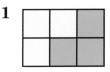

2

3

4
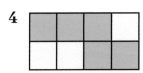

5
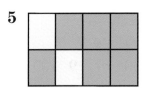

6
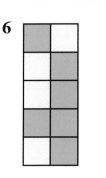

Exercise 19

1 1 can be made from 2 halves.
$$1 = \tfrac{1}{2} + \tfrac{1}{2}$$
   a How many halves in 2?
   b How many halves in 3?
   c How many halves in 4?
   d How many halves in 5?
   e How many halves in 10?

2 1 can be made from 4 quarters.
$$1 = \tfrac{1}{4} + \tfrac{1}{4} + \tfrac{1}{4} + \tfrac{1}{4}$$
   a How many quarters in 2?
   b How many quarters in 3?
   c How many quarters in 4?
   d How many quarters in 5?
   e How many quarters in 10?

3 1 can be made from 5 fifths.
$$1 = \tfrac{1}{5} + \tfrac{1}{5} + \tfrac{1}{5} + \tfrac{1}{5} + \tfrac{1}{5}$$
   a How many fifths in 2?
   b How many fifths in 3?
   c How many fifths in 4?
   d How many fifths in 5?
   e How many fifths in 10?

4 1 can be made from 10 tenths.
$$1 = \tfrac{1}{10} + \tfrac{1}{10} + \tfrac{1}{10} + \tfrac{1}{10} + \tfrac{1}{10}$$
$$+ \tfrac{1}{10} + \tfrac{1}{10} + \tfrac{1}{10} + \tfrac{1}{10} + \tfrac{1}{10}$$
   a How many tenths in 2?
   b How many tenths in 3?
   c How many tenths in 4?
   d How many tenths in 5?
   e How many tenths in 10?

Exercise 20

Write each top heavy fraction as a whole number and a fraction.

1 $\frac{5}{3}$

2 $\frac{4}{3}$

3 $\frac{7}{4}$

4 $\frac{5}{4}$

5 $\frac{6}{4}$

6 $\frac{5}{2}$

7 $\frac{9}{5}$

8 $\frac{12}{7}$

9 $\frac{12}{10}$

10 $\frac{13}{8}$

11 $\frac{13}{10}$

12 $\frac{22}{10}$

13 $\frac{14}{9}$

14 $\frac{16}{8}$

15 $\frac{15}{4}$

Exercise 21

Example
$\frac{1}{4}$ of 8 = 2

1 $\frac{1}{4}$ of 20

2 $\frac{1}{3}$ of 18

3 $\frac{1}{5}$ of 20

4 $\frac{1}{4}$ of 12

5 $\frac{1}{8}$ of 24

6 $\frac{1}{10}$ of 30

7 $\frac{1}{3}$ of 21

8 $\frac{1}{3}$ of 30

9 $\frac{1}{4}$ of 28

10 $\frac{1}{5}$ of 25

11 $\frac{1}{4}$ of 40

12 $\frac{1}{5}$ of 35

13 $\frac{1}{10}$ of 70

14 $\frac{1}{7}$ of 70

15 $\frac{1}{8}$ of 32

Exercise 22

Example
$\frac{1}{4}$ of 20 = 5
$\frac{3}{4}$ of 20 =
$3 \times 5 = 15$

1 $\frac{1}{4}$ of 12
$\frac{3}{4}$ of 12

2 $\frac{1}{5}$ of 20
$\frac{4}{5}$ of 20

3 $\frac{1}{4}$ of 28
$\frac{3}{4}$ of 28

4 $\frac{1}{3}$ of 9
$\frac{2}{3}$ of 9

5 $\frac{1}{10}$ of 30
$\frac{4}{10}$ of 30

6 $\frac{3}{5}$ of 15

7 $\frac{2}{3}$ of 30

8 $\frac{7}{10}$ of 20

9 $\frac{5}{6}$ of 36

10 $\frac{7}{8}$ of 64

Example

5 divided by 3 is $\frac{5}{3} = 1\frac{2}{3}$

Exercise 23

Write the answers in fractions.

1 7 divided by 5

2 8 divided by 5

3 7 divided by 4

4 8 divided by 6

5 15 divided by 11

6 $5 \div 4$

7 $8 \div 7$

8 $12 \div 7$

9 $13 \div 9$

10 $20 \div 12$

11 $9 \div 4$

12 $13 \div 4$

13 $15 \div 4$

14 $18 \div 5$

15 $19 \div 7$

Example

$\frac{3}{6}$ is the same as $\frac{1}{2}$

$\frac{3}{6} = \frac{1}{2}$

Exercise 24

Write down the fraction shaded for each shape.

1

$$\frac{6}{8} = \frac{}{4}$$

2

$$\frac{}{4} = \frac{}{16}$$

3

4

5

6

7

You need a calculator for this exercise.

Example

$\frac{3}{4} = 3 \div 4 = 0.75$

Example

$\frac{3}{4}$ of £20 = £15

£20 ÷ 4 = £5

£5 × 3 = £15

Exercise 25

Change these fractions to decimals.

1 $\frac{1}{4}$

2 $\frac{2}{5}$

3 $\frac{4}{5}$

4 $\frac{7}{10}$

5 $\frac{3}{5}$

6 $\frac{6}{8}$

7 $\frac{15}{20}$

8 $\frac{18}{20}$

9 $\frac{5}{8}$

10 $\frac{6}{10}$

11 $\frac{12}{16}$

12 $\frac{75}{100}$

13 Use your answers to write down 4 fractions that are equal to $\frac{3}{4}$.

Exercise 26

Find these fractions of money. You can use a calculator. Remember that ⟨ **0.5** ⟩ means 50 p not 5 p!

1 $\frac{3}{4}$ of 24 p

2 $\frac{3}{4}$ of £12

3 $\frac{3}{4}$ of £30

4 $\frac{3}{4}$ of 96 p

5 $\frac{3}{4}$ of £2.84

6 $\frac{3}{4}$ of £24.72

7 $\frac{2}{5}$ of £15

8 $\frac{3}{5}$ of £20

9 $\frac{4}{5}$ of £17.50

10 $\frac{2}{5}$ of 95 p

11 $\frac{3}{5}$ of £2.50

12 $\frac{4}{5}$ of £12.50

13 $\frac{2}{5}$ of £16

14 $\frac{3}{5}$ of £24

15 $\frac{3}{10}$ of 70 p

16 $\frac{7}{10}$ of £1.20

Money

pounds (£) → ×100 → pence (p)

pence (p) → ÷100 → pounds (£)

Examples

£3 → ×100 → 300p
£3.40 → ×100 → 340p
£0.50 → ×100 → 50p

216p → ÷100 → £2.16
500p → ÷100 → £5.00
95p → ÷100 → £0.95

Exercise 27

Convert these pounds into pence.

1	£4	**6**	£1.24
2	£10.49	**7**	£1.90
3	£3.20	**8**	£10
4	£0.63	**9**	£16.01
5	£6.00	**10**	£6.01

Common metric units of length

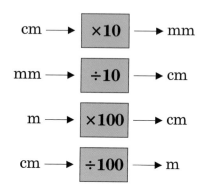

cm → ×10 → mm

mm → ÷10 → cm

m → ×100 → cm

cm → ÷100 → m

Examples

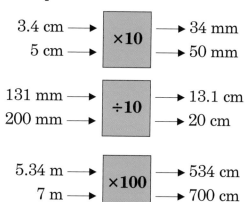

3.4 cm → ×10 → 34 mm
5 cm → ×10 → 50 mm

131 mm → ÷10 → 13.1 cm
200 mm → ÷10 → 20 cm

5.34 m → ×100 → 534 cm
7 m → ×100 → 700 cm

349 cm → ÷100 → 3.49 m
25 cm → ÷100 → 0.25 m

Exercise 28

Convert these pence into pounds.

1	315 p	**6**	14 p
2	756 p	**7**	29 p
3	1054 p	**8**	5000 p
4	100 p	**9**	150 p
5	650 p	**10**	87 p

Exercise 29

Convert these cm to mm.

1	6.5 cm	**6**	100 cm
2	12.8 cm	**7**	142.1 cm
3	14.2 cm	**8**	1.2 cm
4	16.4 cm	**9**	0.9 cm
5	0.5 cm	**10**	426 cm

Exercise 30

Convert these mm to cm.

1 126 mm

2 42 mm

3 100 mm

4 10 mm

5 207 mm

6 186 mm

7 365 mm

8 66 mm

9 200 mm

10 500 mm

Exercise 31

Convert these m to cm.

1 25 m

2 102 m

3 3.65 m

4 9.02 m

5 12.20 m

6 79 m

7 1000 m

8 1 m

9 4.75 m

10 2.50 m

Exercise 32

Convert these cm to m.

1 16 400 cm

2 2500 cm

3 100 cm

4 150 cm

5 125 cm

6 396 cm

7 1441 cm

8 1201 cm

9 370 cm

10 1000 cm

Exercise 33

Convert these units to the units in brackets.

1 £1.25   (p)

2 £0.70   (p)

3 2.50 m   (cm)

4 10.75 m   (cm)

5 250 cm   (m)

6 250 p   (£)

7 350 cm   (m)

8 1000 mm   (cm)

9 500 cm   (m)

10 10 mm   (cm)